Funny Side Up

*A Southern Girl's Guide to
Love, Laughter, and Money*

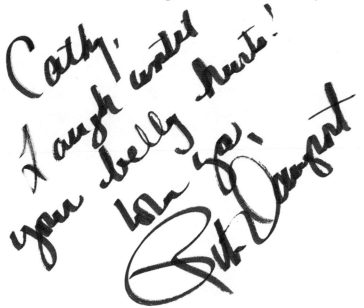

Also by Rita Davenport

Sourdough Cookery
De Grazia and Mexican Cookery
Making Time, Making Money

Praise for Rita Davenport
and *Funny Side Up*

"Rita and I have so much in common. We both hail from Tennessee, raised in families so poor neither of us had an indoor pot to piddle in. Both of us were tiny back-country blondes with great big dreams, girls who grew up in poverty but never saw it as anything but a minor inconvenience. We both shared bushels of determination, and neither of us was ever willing to accept what folks told us we couldn't do. Rita shattered the proverbial glass ceiling, and used the shards to make the cutest li'l sequin dress. I love the girl! And you'll love *Funny Side Up!*"
    —Dolly Parton, entertainer

"Rita Davenport's impact on the world is unparalleled, and seen through the hearts of the thousands of people whose lives are fabulous today because of her love and guidance."
    —Sharon Lechter, coauthor of *Three Feet From Gold* and *Rich Dad Poor Dad*

"Inside each person is the seed of their potential—their acorn. Within your acorn lie all your possibilities, your 'greatest gifts,' as my friend Rita Davenport puts it, just awaiting your commitment to grow them. I have seen Rita awaken the potential in many people who are successful leaders today. Let her inspire and guide you as she has so many thousands of others!"
    —Jim Cathcart, bestselling author of *The Acorn Principle*

"Rita Davenport is a true leader who has inspired others throughout her career with her great insights into how to live a successful life—and how to have fun doing it."
    —Tom Hopkins, author of *How to Master the Art of Selling*

"If you are ready to experience vastly more sunshine in every aspect of your life, read my friend Rita's brilliant new book *Funny Side Up*. Even better, read it, absorb it, use its wisdom in your life—and share it with those you love and bring the sunshine into their lives, too!"
   —Mark Victor Hansen, co-creator of the
   bestselling *Chicken Soup for the Soul* series

"Rita Davenport has been there and done that. Raising herself from rags to riches, she had her own successful television talk show and became the top executive of a large worldwide company. She is a natural storyteller with a highly motivational message. There's an old saying: Give a person a fish and you feed them for a day; teach them how to fish and you feed them for life. Rita's book teaches you how to fish! Read and be rewarded."
   —Calvin LeHew, founder of The Factory at
   Franklin and coauthor of *Flying High*

"Rita Davenport is an icon in the self-empowerment movement. Her insightful, entertaining, and heartfelt words will help you to reach deep within yourself, expand your vision of what is possible, soar to new heights, and live a life of meaning and significance."
   —Les Brown, CPAE, bestselling author of *Live
   Your Dreams*, National Speaker's Association,
   Hall of Fame Speaker, Toastmasters
   International Golden Gavel Award

"A remarkable collection of insights that teaches with humor how generosity, humility, and thankfulness will take your business and personal relationships to the next level. You'll be moved, uplifted, and educated by a talented teller of real-life tales about what's really important in life and how to measure success. You'll find yourself laughing, crying, and nodding in agreement."
   —Jeanne Robertson, CSP, CPAE, past president,
   National Speakers Association

"This priceless gem speaks to the heart of true success and fulfillment. By chasing our passion, not our pension, we all can receive the gift that comes from knowing that all life—present and future—has been nurtured by our individual contributions."
— Denis Waitley, author, *The Seeds of Greatness*

"Don't waste a minute of your time reading Rita Davenport's new book... *unless* you are totally committed to being an even more effective salesperson, leader, and individual! You'll laugh, you'll cry, you'll be energized and inspired, but you'll *never* be bored by Rita's amazing wit, wisdom, and wonderful true stories. Few people can hold a live audience the way Rita can, and even fewer people can put that skill into a book—but Rita has done it!"
— Joel Weldon, CSP, CPAE, award-winning
speaker, recipient of the Golden Gavel and
2006 Legend of the Speaking Profession

"In these days of pop-up celebrities and twenty-five-cent teletherapists, Rita Davenport is the real deal. This lady has seen it all, done it all, and knows what she's talking about. Curl up in your favorite chair and spend a few hours with one of the most inspiring people I have ever met. She'll warm your heart, make you laugh, and touch your soul—and you will never be the same!"
— Connie Podesta, CSP, CPAE, author of
10 Ways to Stand Out from the Crowd

"Rita Davenport has such a depth of experience and wealth of good ideas that I listen to whatever she says and read whatever she writes. Her ability to teach great truths with warmth and humor make her a powerful communicator. I've learned from her, and you will, too, if you read her excellent new book. I recommend it."
— Mark Sanborn, CSP, CPAE, award-winning
speaker and author of *The Fred Factor* and
You Don't Need a Title to be a Leader

"No one I know in the world of motivation and personal growth comes close to having Rita Davenport's gift of being world-wise brilliant and side-splittingly funny at the same time. The strategic life lessons she doles out in *Funny Side Up* are so well-laced with laughter that you get the message and learn something powerful and important before you even realize it. An important book—beautifully entertaining and enlightening!"

—Shad Helmstetter, Ph.D., bestselling author
of *What to Say When You Talk to Yourself*

"Rita Davenport is one of the most powerfully authentic people I have ever met. In a world full of smoke and mirrors, she needs none; her wisdom and insight are among the best of the best. Be careful—before you know it, she will change your life!"

—Keith Kochner, founder, Mentorship
Mastery and Mentorfish.com

"I have known Rita for more than thirty-five years. She is funny, charming, honest, self-effacing, ambitious, caring, heartfelt, and fabulously successful… and she has dedicated her life to helping, inspiring, and supporting others to become their best selves. Pick up this book and join the millions who love and adore Rita. You will be blessed to have her in your life!"

—Dian Thomas, television personality and
bestselling author of *Roughing It Easy*

"*Funny Side Up* is one of the most inspirational and well-crafted books I've read in a long time. Rita Davenport, who has literally gone from rags to riches, has a compelling story that will motivate you to become the person you would like to be. And don't let her mellifluous Tennessee accent fool you for a moment: she is a powerful and eloquent speaker who can evoke emotions from deep sadness to soaring inspiration—and in the next heartbeat have you laughing so hard you can barely breathe."

—Dr. Art Mollen, author, *Dr. Mollen's Anti-Aging Diet*

"Rita Davenport blew into my life when I was losing myself. I saved my grocery money to buy her audiocassettes, and my car became a rolling University of Rita. Through her I learned to love myself, which is what FLYing is all about: Finally Loving Yourself. Rita's message touched my heart. She changed my life with her words, and she'll change yours, too."

—Marla "FlyLady" Cilley, coauthor of the
  New York Times bestseller *Body Clutter:*
  Love Your Body, Love Yourself

"Funny, charming, honest, self-effacing, caring, and fabulously successful—this lady walks her talk as she leads with her heart. I've been friends with Rita over thirty years. After a great deal of prodding, she has decided to put her story down on paper. I'm sure you'll be as thrilled as I was when you read her remarkable book. The message and tools in this book will help to improve not only your organization and your career, but your entire life."

—Joe Larson, CSP, CPAE, former president of National
  Speakers Association and winner of the Cavett Award

"Rita Davenport has more energy than Hoover Dam on Red Bull. She has enjoyed multimedia success and has inspired thousands along her journey. And the motivational kick-in-the-butt from Rita's live speaking engagements make Knute Rockne and General George S. Patton seem like pacifists. Rita Davenport could write the *alphabet* and sell more copies than *Gone with the Wind*. I will be the first to buy a copy of Rita's new book... and I will be the first to charge her $34.95 for this quote."

—Dave "Morning Mayor" Pratt, host,
  KUPD's *Dave Pratt in the Morning*

Funny Side Up

A Southern Girl's Guide to
Love, Laughter, and Money

by Rita Davenport

with John David Mann

SUCCESS

Published by SUCCESS.

SUCCESS

200 Swisher Road
Lake Dallas, Texas 75065
Toll-free: 866-SUCCESS (782-2377)
www.SUCCESS.com

SUCCESS is a registered trademark and *SUCCESS* magazine is
a trademark of SUCCESS Partners.

Printed in the United States of America.

Book design by Sam Watson

ISBN 978-1-935944-43-0

SPECIAL SALES
SUCCESS books are available at special discounts for bulk
purchase for sales promotions and premiums. Special editions,
including personalized covers, excerpts of existing books,
and corporate imprints, can be created in large quantities for
special needs. For more information, contact Special Markets,
SUCCESS, sales@success.com.

Dedication

This book is dedicated to you, the reader, and to my family, friends, teachers, mastermind group, staff, and peers, with great joy, appreciation, and love. You all know who you are and you're way too humble to need recognition.

To Mama and Daddy and my brother Ray: from where you sit in Heaven, I'm sure you can see how much I truly miss you.

To my sister, Euphiazene, and my brother-in-law, Lucion: you both taught me to listen with my heart and speak from my soul.

To my husband, David: everything I am and will be, I owe to you.

To my sons, Michael and Scott, two of my greatest teachers: I love you.

To my granddaughters, Reese and Claire Ray: you are the light of my life. Remember, it costs nothing to dream—but everything if you don't.

To anyone else who finds yourself in a place in life where you are looking for your *why*, when the question of *why* seems unanswerable: you are never alone.

Now the journey begins, and I get to share all you've taught me…

Contents

Foreword by Darren Hardy

I may not know you personally, but I know something about you, maybe even a few things.

For example, I know that you were born. I also know that *when* you were born, you were a powderkeg of potential, a supernova of big dreams, boundless imagination, and daring intentions.

How do I know that? Because this is true of every one of us. On the way to launching us into life, a lion's share of possibility is poured into each of us, along with the gifts, the talents, and the passion to bring it to fruition.

And then it begins.

As growth gets under way, circumstances crowd in around us, sometimes so chokingly close that they make it hard to breathe. Disappointments and discouragements take root and grow, competing for sunlight and nutrients with the vines of our own best aspirations. We become singed by myriad slights and burned by the hurts of painful experiences.

I've written a number of books on developing one's self personally, because the subject fascinates me and is instilled in every fiber of my being. I've studied successful people for nearly twenty years, and I've known hundreds of high-profile people who have achieved big dreams. I've learned that dreams can be challenging, can sometimes feel intimidating, and are *always* worth the SUCCESS they can bring. And I've learned that dreams are fragile things, too. So many people have had their dreams knocked right out of them.

Perhaps that describes you.

If so, if there is even a part of you that yearns to "be more, have more, learn more, and earn more so you could share more," then you've come to the right place.

By the way, I put those words in quotation marks—"be more, have more, learn more, and earn more so you can share more"—because they are not mine but are one of a thousand trademark phrases from the remarkable spirit known to the world as Rita Davenport.

Rita is one of the most successful women I've ever known, but possibly not for the reasons you might think.

Yes, she has led an amazing career in broadcast, interviewing hundreds of celebrities on her own television show. Yes, she has been a bestselling author. (I don't know any other authors offhand who have penned bestsellers about time management and about sourdough cooking.) Yes, she has served as president at the helm of a company with an astonishing success story. She is as powerful a leader as she is hilarious, as personable as she is dynamic and unstoppable.

The reason I say Rita is one of the most successful people I know is that she has inspired so many to step out of their limitations and to become what they always knew, deep down, they could become. I know that's why she's written this book, and I suspect that's why you're reading it.

As you browse the pages ahead, I hope you will remember something.

Rita's story is so engaging and entertaining that it's easy to just sit back and enjoy the ride. Her journey— from Tennessee poverty to Arizona fame, from a speech defect to the national arena where she became one of the most sought-after motivational speakers in America (with Southern twang alive and well)—is a wild ride indeed, and seeing it leap from the page is *almost* as funny as hearing her tell it live from the stage.

But while you're being entertained, don't let the point of it all slip past you unnoticed. Because there's a method to her madness. Rita isn't here just to tell her story. She's telling you what she's done for only one reason: to show you *what's possible.*

Rita does a lot of things well, but she does one thing *exceptionally* well: she inspires people to be their best. She has done this for literally millions of people. Now she's here to do it for you, and I'm honored to be the one making the introductions.

Dear Reader—please meet my friend Rita Davenport.

Rita—my new friend Dear Reader.

I know the two of you will get along famously.

Darren Hardy
New York Times Bestselling Author
and Publisher of *SUCCESS* magazine
www.darrenhardy.com

A Word from Your Copilot

A few years ago a friend and I wrote a book titled *The Go-Giver*, and in the story there was a character referred to as "the keynote speaker." This woman was an amazing speaker, with an extraordinary capacity to be both profound and hilarious at the same time, and she had touched millions of lives with her story. When the protagonist, Joe, hears her speak about authenticity, it signals a turning point in the story.

We named the speaker "Debra Davenport"—and that was *not* a coincidence.

When Bob Burg and I wrote *The Go-Giver* I'd already known Rita (not Debra) Davenport for nearly a decade. I met her first in the nineties, when I interviewed her for a magazine cover about phenomenally successful female company presidents. But by that time I had already known her *by reputation* for many years. It seemed that everyone I knew and everyone I talked to had heard of Rita, most had heard her speak, and all had some variation of the same thing to say:

"Oh, Rita Davenport—I *love* her!"

The outpouring of affection and admiration that seemed to follow this woman around made me wonder if she was something like Mother Teresa. When I met her, I found out: yes, she was exactly like that—if you can picture Mother Teresa with lightning-fast and screamingly funny delivery in an outrageous Southern twang ... and wearing terrific outfits.

Fast forward.

In mid-2011 I get a call from my friend Reed Bilbray, at

SUCCESS, who wants to know if I have some time to work on a book project with them. Alas, I reply, I am really and truly jammed, half a dozen projects on my plate, couldn't possibly take on another one, very sorry, love to but no can do.

Then he tells me it's a book with Rita.

And that's that. (I can't very well say no to a character out of one of my own books, can I?)

It's hard to describe just what a pleasure it has been to listen to Rita tell her life story and then weave the bits and pieces of it, together with her perspectives on life and living, into the book you're now holding in your hands.

The reason I'm excited to see this book finished and on its way out into the world is that I already know what kind of impact it will have on people's lives. Rita has a sort of Socratic Midas touch. Socrates asked his students questions until they found the answers inside themselves. Rita does something like that, only she interacts with people until they discover the *gold* inside themselves. And when she talks about "a rich life," she's not just talking about financial abundance, but about the abundant richness of human experience, accomplishment, connection, fulfillment, and love.

Every phone call I've had with Rita ends the same way: the last words I hear as I'm about to hang up are, "Love ya!"

That's how she ends every phone call with *everyone*. And she's not kidding.

Love ya too, Rita.

John David Mann

Before We Get Started...

... let's put this one right out on the table: I talk funny.

Not that what I *say* is always funny. Although I do put a lot of importance on humor, because I think it helps us keep things in perspective, and even when it doesn't succeed in doing that, at least it keeps us sane. And if it doesn't do *that*, it still makes us laugh—and laughing is good for you. It's a proven scientific fact that laughter increases endorphins[1], lowers blood pressure[2], helps regulate cortisol and epinephrine, the stress hormones, and boosts immune function.[3] It also causes weight loss and raises sex hormones. Okay, I just made that last part up. But it *could* be true. Makes sense to me, and until there's science that disproves it, I'm goin' with it!

But no, what I mean is, I *talk* funny.

I was born and raised in a Tennessee home so poor we had no indoor plumbing, and unless you were born and raised there too, I don't talk the way you talk. As an adult, when I moved to Phoenix, Arizona, and pursued a master's degree in child development, I worked with young children at the college daycare center. Soon after I arrived, parents were calling the program administrator and saying, "Uh, Dr. Ferrone? This is really strange, but ... our children are speaking *Southern*." Imagine that! I do not know how that happened.

On top of that thick-as-molasses Shake 'n' Bake accent, as a child I had a speech defect. My favorite dress was one my aunt had sewn for me out of some big old fifty-pound feed sacks when I was six. I went around the neighborhood bragging about it, except I couldn't say *feed sack* and instead it came out *theed thack*, so for the next few years, to the people of Flat Rock, Tennessee, I was known as Theedthack. Those years are behind me now, nobody calls me Theedthack anymore and, while there are those who might disagree with this next statement, I no longer have a speech defect. But you could put me in a basin and scrub me all you want and, thankfully, the Tennessee in me is still never coming out.

My point is this: I talk Southern.

Think Dolly Parton, then speed it up from 33⅓ to 78 rpm and take away the guitar, and you've pretty much got me. Which is interesting, because I once dated the guy who ended up marrying Dolly Parton. I never understood what he saw in her. I'm kidding, of course. Dolly came to Phoenix one time and said she wanted to meet me and offered to be on my television show. I think it was because I was one of the few girls her guy had dated before her, and she was curious to find out just who I was. I said, "Well, Dolly, you're probably wondering what he saw in me. I'll save you the trouble of trying to figure it out and just come out and tell you the truth: I wore a padded bra." She said, "I figured. He told me that's what he guessed." I said, "Well I'm glad he wasn't naïve!" Dolly and I had us a good time together. But we'll come back to Dolly Parton in another chapter, because she has a story to tell here, too.

The reason I mention the speech defect, the hillbilly accent, and the mile-a-minute resting rate of my natural speech patterns is that it all makes this fact very clear: from the very start, God was playing tricks on me. Why do I say that? Because in the course of my life, as you'll see, I eventually discovered that He had put me here on this earth to be a public speaker.

Hello? A public speaker—with a speech defect? And who talks Southern?

It's a little bit like hiding Easter eggs. I was given a gift—only after being hard boiled and painted with all kinds of spiffy colors, the darn thing was hidden long before I even knew it was there, and hidden so well I nearly missed it altogether.

Now you might think this book is about my life story. And yes, there will be bits and pieces of my story in here, at least enough so you can get an idea of who this person is talking to you from these pages. But this book isn't really about me: *it's about you.*

And right here, this is the part where you come in. We'll get to my story in a bit. For the moment, I'm more interested in getting to *your* story.

Chapter 1

WHY ARE YOU HERE?

Why *are* you here? I know there's a reason. None of us are here by accident. What is your gift? And what are you supposed to do with it?

I fervently believe that every single one of us is sent into this world with a unique purpose. Not only that: I believe we are each sent into this world with a purpose *and* with all the talent we need to fulfill that purpose. And by *everyone* I mean *you*. But you've got to find those gifts within yourself—and you have to have the courage, the passion, and the belief in yourself to let them shine through.

Oh, and if you're not sure you know what your purpose is, don't worry, because you were born with clues built right in. If you played hide-and-seek when you were a kid, remember what your friends would say when you started getting close to finding the right hiding place? "You're getting warm." Finding your purpose is a lot like that. When you start getting closer, you get warm. And when you get real close, you get hot. It's called *passion*.

It Starts with Passion

Every recipe has its key ingredient. If you're going to bake a cake, you start with flour. To make an omelet, you start with eggs. If you want to create a rich, fulfilling life, the ingredient you start with is *passion*. A rich life is one where you cannot wait to get up in the morning and set about whatever it is you're doing that day.

A friend of mine was shopping at a food store one day and the clerk, a friendly young man, got to talking with him. "Do you mind if I ask, what do you do for work?"

"I'm a writer," my friend replied.

"Really. Do you like it?"

"I don't just like it," said my friend, "I *love* it."

The young man stopped what he was doing, put down the package he was wrapping, and stared at my friend. "*Really*," he said. "I have to tell you, I ask that question to every customer who'll talk to me. I've asked it more than a hundred times. You know how many of those people told me they *love* what they do? One ... *you*. That's it!"

Can you imagine that? One person in a hundred wakes up genuinely looking forward to the day's work. That's a tragedy. On the other hand, it's also an opportunity, because you get to *be* that one person in a hundred, and when you are, you become a magnet to the other ninety-nine. Let me explain how that works.

It's been said that enthusiasm is the presence of God within. In fact, the word itself comes from the Greek *theos* for God and *en-* for *within*. But you don't have wait to be struck down on the road to Damascus or hit by a bolt of inspiration from above. The passion of genuine enthusiasm is an energy you can generate yourself. How? Simple: by focusing your time, effort, and energy on those ideas, activities and pursuits that get you excited. Hey, it's not rocket science.

Stay with me, though, because there's more here than meets the eye. When you feed your soul by spending time on things you love, that you are excited about, your enthusiasm becomes contagious. Being around someone who's passionate about what they're doing rubs off on other people. It catches like a wildfire (the good kind) and warms them. It makes them want to be around you more and gravitate to that positive energy you're exuding. You become a magnet for that positivity—for greatness—and it's wonderful. I want you to think for a moment about the people you've known or respected who had a true, inspired passion for what they were doing in life and the journey they were on. It makes you feel good inside, doesn't it? Empowered? Energized?

Do you see where this is leading? You'll never accomplish the things you're capable of and live your life to the fullest entirely on your own. It takes a support team of others who buy in to what you're up to. (We'll talk more about *that* in chapter 9, because it's a crucial piece of the whole picture.) So how do you find those people? You don't have to: they will find you. The people, resources, situations, and circumstances you'll need to fulfill your purpose will all be *drawn* to you—so long as you're *on* purpose.

I've often been asked, "How is it you always seem so enthusiastic? How do you get that way?" Let me explain how this works: you don't *get* that way. You have to *start* that way. Successful people don't gradually become excited about what they're doing after they've been doing it a while and it starts to show some results. They don't start feeling the passion once the world recognizes them for what they're doing, or after their idea or their pursuit starts generating some reward. That's not the way it works. *First* you find your passion for who you are, for where you are and what you're up to, and *then* the success you're seeking becomes gravitationally drawn toward you.

"But what if I just don't have that passion to start with?" you ask? Don't worry: *you do*. You may have misplaced it, or forgotten it, but trust me, you've got it. And it's important to find it—because you'll never work a day in your life unless you'd rather be doing something else.

Here, I'll prove it to you.

How You Started Out

Do you consider yourself athletic? How would you rate yourself, say, as a swimmer? Average, below average, maybe a little above average? So-so? Terrible? Well, I've got news for you: whether you know it or not, you are a world-class super-Olympic gold medal swimmer.

I'm not kidding.

You know how I know that? Because I took anatomy, physiology, bacteriology, and chemistry in college, as part of my science minor. And here's what I learned: we all start out the same way, as tiny sperm cells. In order for you to be born, assuming your daddy had an average sperm count, you had to have out-swum some 200,000 other sperm. And it was uphill all the way.

Now, I do not know what motivated you, but that little tail was wiggling like mad, and you were screaming, "Out of my way! Out of my way! I want to teach school! I want to dance! I want to be in real estate! I want to be a journalist!" or whatever it was you were screaming at the top of your little sperm voice.

You know who the losers are in life? It's simple, and I'll tell you how you can recognize them. They're not as tall as you are. In fact, they're not even as tall as the thickness of one of your eyelashes. They're the sperm cells you left behind in the Fallopian dust. You haven't heard much from them lately, have you? No. But out of 200,000 (or 600,000, if your daddy was above average), here you are.

Do you suppose it was just an accident that you made it across that ovarian finish line? Just a random thing? You suppose the other 199,999 sperm were all way ahead of you, but they just had the bad luck of stubbing their little toes on the last lap and stumbling? Nuh-uh. They lost because you were out in front, pure and simple. You were unstoppable. You know why? Because you had something that would not allow you to be anyone but the sperm at the front of the pack.

It was no accident. You had purpose. You were *on* purpose. And you know what? You're still that same person today. That's all still in you, raring to go and eager to shine, and it's time you *let* it.

The World Steps Aside for Those Who Know Where They're Going

Have you ever been in a public place when you desperately needed to use the bathroom? Imagine this scene: you stride into a busy, crowded corridor full of people milling around, all going different directions, all with things on their minds, none of them paying you any attention. But you really, *really* have to go to the bathroom. You know what happens? Even though you don't say a word, when people catch the look in your eyes, let me tell you, they'll step aside and let you through. I'm speaking from experience here.

All of life is like that: if you really, really have to do something, anything, people will step aside and let you at it. But you've got to decide where you're going and have a seriously intense drive to do it. You have to be clear about your intentions. You've got to get your *ask* in gear!

Og Mandino, best-selling author of *The Greatest Salesman in the World*, once shared this story with me:

> A young man traveled to India because he'd heard there was a wise old man living up on a mountain who held the secret of success. He climbed all the way to the mountain's peak, where he found the old man gazing out at the world. "Sir," he said, "could you teach me the secret to success? What do I have to do to be successful?"
>
> The old man looked at him and said, "Son, come with me," and they climbed down the mountain until they reached a river.
>
> Suddenly the old man grabbed the young man by the back of his shirt collar, plunged his head

under the water, and held him there, kicking and thrashing, until the poor kid felt he was on the verge of drowning. At that point, the guru pulled him out and hauled him onto the riverbank, where he sat, spitting, coughing, and trembling. The older man waited until the young man had recovered enough to listen, and he said, "Son, when you want to succeed as bad as you wanted to breathe just now, that's when you will have achievement in your life."

When you want something so bad you feel like you'll drown without it, and you put your whole heart and soul into it, you will become great at it, and people will be drawn to you.

If You Don't Have the Skills, You'll *Gain* the Skills

In 1982, a seventy-seven-year-old great-grandmother named Editha Merrill had triple bypass surgery. Technically speaking, she did not survive the surgery—that is, she fulfilled the clinical definition of death while on the operating table. However, the surgical team was able to resuscitate her, and she pulled through.

When she came out from under anesthesia, her best friend was standing there holding her hand. "Editha, we almost lost you," she said gently. "Honey, you almost didn't make it. They told us you actually *died* in surgery!"

Merrill looked up at her and said, "Well, why *did* I make it? I've got nothing to do and nothing to live for. My husband's been dead for twelve years. My son lives miles away. I'm all alone. Why didn't I just go ahead and die?"

"Editha," her friend replied firmly, "God's not through with you yet. I don't know what it is, but there's something you're supposed to do."

A little more than a year later, Editha's friend's words took on a prophetic meaning. While she and three neighbors were taking a short flight from Phoenix to Sedona in a little four-seater, one of the group, a man named Bruce Turner, suffered a heart attack from which he would never recover. As shocking as that was, there was a detail that made it even more frightening: Bruce was also their pilot.

Although Editha happened to be sitting in the copilot's seat, she was no expert pilot. In fact, she was no kind of pilot at all. She had no more experience behind the controls of an aircraft than you or I. But what was she going to do? She flew the plane. With a flight instructor on the ground talking her down, Editha piloted the craft for two hours, including a rough patch through some clouds that cut their visibility to zero. When she landed back at Luke Air Force Base two hours later, the entire staff of the base was outside screaming and yelling, waving handkerchiefs and flags (so they would know which way to run if the plane didn't land safely, I guess), as the little Piper Cherokee floated in and made its perfect three-point landing. Editha cut the engine and the plane rolled over onto the grass. The emergency crew drove up and the driver stuck his thumb up in an A-OK sign of victory. Editha grinned and echoed his gesture, sticking her thumb up in the air as well.[4]

I don't know about you, but if I were in her place, I would have been *sucking* my thumb. One of my friends said, "I'd have had rope burns from my rosary." When I told my friend Joe Garagiola, the Major League catcher and baseball announcer, what had happened with Editha, he said, "Rita, if that were me, I would have had a laundry problem you wouldn't have believed!"

I had a chance to talk with Jack Seeley, the flight instructor who talked Editha through that flight and landing, and I learned from him that the last time she had been in an airplane had been fifty years earlier. "Rita," Jack said, "if I'd known that the woman I was talking to on that radio was seventy-eight years old, I'll be honest with you, I'm not sure I even would have tried to help. I'd have figured, no way would she be able to fly that airplane, let alone land it." Good thing he didn't ask her how old she was. (See? There's a reason it's not wise to ask a woman her age. Besides, a woman who'll tell you her age will lie about other things, too.)

Editha Merrill's friend was right: she had a purpose. That was the reason she didn't die on the operating table. She was supposed to land that airplane. *She* was supposed to save those other people's lives.

Did she have the skills to do it? No, she sure didn't. But she acquired them, and pretty darn fast, too. If she could do that, at seventy-eight, do you think you can learn the skills you'll need to fulfill *your* purpose?

Because let me tell you something: you have a purpose, or else you would not be alive today. You want to live a rich life? Find out what your purpose is, get crystal clear on it, and throw yourself into it.

When I say you have a talent, you may question that. But don't—because you do! I questioned it about myself for years. I didn't intend to do what I've done for a living. I intended to be Tina Turner. Unfortunately God didn't give me Tina Turner's voice. (He had already given it to her. He also knew I wouldn't have put up with Ike for a second.) I got over it.

What do you love to do? What are you passionate about? Whatever that is, dive into it and get good at it. No, get *great* at it.

No Compromise

Once you discover what your purpose is, you can't let anyone else tell you differently. I'm not saying you should stick your fingers in your ears and close your mind off to other people's perspective. Sometimes people see things in you that you don't see in yourself. But when it comes to the core of your being, the very soul of who you are and why you're here? *Your* voice is the only one you can trust.

When people tell you that you can't do it, give yourself the gift of tunnel vision. Don't listen to them. Listen to yourself, because you've got the answers within you right now.

You've already got everything you need within you to be outrageously successful. Everything. A scientist once told me something I thought was fascinating: you have the atomic components and energy within you that's equivalent to the force of an atomic bomb. It's a question of how those elements are focused. I said this once in a speech. Afterward, a woman came up to me and said, "Do I really have the energy within me, like an atomic bomb?" I said, "Yes, ma'am, you do." She said, "Well, you know, I thought I was having a little gas, but I didn't know it was that serious." Funny what people hear from what you say, isn't it?

I interviewed the Oscar-winning actor Dustin Hoffman once years ago at a press junket, and he told us he had a list of people who had all told him, back when he was starting out and struggling to get a foot in the door of the acting world, that he was ugly, he was scrawny, he sounded stupid, and wasn't ever going to amount to anything. "I keep that list with me," he said. "You know why? To remind me that other people's opinions are just that."

All the people on that list knew, I mean they *knew*, beyond all shadow of the slightest doubt, that Dustin Hoffman would never make it as an actor. Other people's opinions. But Hoffman made sure to stay in control of the one opinion that mattered: his own. That's worked out pretty well for him, don't you think? It will for you, too.

Are you every bit as successful, right now, as you know you could be? If not, what's holding you back? I'll tell you what's holding you back: other people's opinions. You've been handed a script that's been programmed into you by family members, friends, teachers, and all kinds of people you've come into contact with, and you're following the script. You've bought into their story. You're thinking, "Yeah, I'll never be able to do that, it's just not something I'm capable of," because somebody else told you that.

I know, because I was handed a script, too. (I'll tell you all about it in the next few chapters.) We all were. But that story isn't your story, it's a story others made up for you. They weren't necessarily trying to ruin your life. In fact, the chances are good they were only doing their best to help, doing what they thought would be in your best interests. I've raised two sons, and I know how tempting it is to look at someone you love trying to figure out what they're supposed to do with this thing called *their life*, and think, "Here, let me help you with that…"

But good intentions or not, they don't know your story. I don't know what your purpose in life is. Who does? *You* do.

It's a simple three-step process:

First: Find out what it is you want to do. What you were put here to do. What speaks to your soul.

Second: Start doing it. Go for it. Throw yourself into it, body mind and soul.

And third: Keep doing it no matter what. Don't compromise. The only time you fail is when you quit!

Life Is Choice

Life is all about choices. Life itself *is* choice. That's what distinguishes things that are alive: they make choices. Plants grow toward the sunlight. Dogs run after the sticks you throw. People pursue careers and create circumstances.

Editha Merrill had a choice. She could have said, "We're doomed, no way can I fly an airplane—I'm seventy-eight, for Heaven's sake, and I've never even touched one of those controls before!" Or she could make a different choice. She chose to land that darned airplane. Dustin Hoffman had a choice too. We all do.

This may be hard to hear (or, if you're a more visual person, hard to *read*), but humor me and just take it on, for a moment, as a what-if-this-is-true, a possibility to consider: *You are where you are, right now, because this is where you've chosen to be.* You can blame all kinds of people conditions and circumstances, but even in those situations where it might seem like you had no choice whatsoever, you are still given a free-will choice about how those people and circumstances will affect you, and about where you go from that point forward. That is a gift we all have. You are where you are because of the choices you've made, whether you've made them with full intention and your eyes wide open, or made them sort of by default, backing into the corners of your life because you didn't think there was any other way to go. You can think of them as active choices versus passive choices—and making active choices has it all beat, hands down.

In fact, for me that is the definition of genuine success itself: *success is living every day the way you choose.* It is living with the clear understanding that you are making your own choices, and embracing those choices fully.

You've probably heard it said that success is not a destination, it's a journey. Well, yeah … but not just *any* journey! Walking over to the corner for a pack of gum is a journey, but I'm not sure that's a very vivid picture of *success.*

No, success is that unique journey where you spend each day living your authentic life, being your authentic self, in hot pursuit of the very reason you were put on the planet in the first place.

My Life in a Nutshell

Here are the simple facts of my life. We'll get into some details here and there later on, but while I've still got your attention I thought it would be polite to give you the general lay of the land.

I started out as a sperm cell. (I think we've covered that part!)

Next, I was born into a very poor family and grew up in Flat Rock, Tennessee. Like I said, no indoor plumbing. We'd have to go out to the street to fetch water, and when it was time to give that water back, we'd go out the other way, to the outhouse. My sister, Euphiazene, was eight years older than I. (She got married at the age of fourteen, when I was just six, started a family four years later at eighteen, and recently celebrated her sixty-second wedding anniversary.) My brother Ray came along two years after I did. All the way through school, until I left home myself, I slept in one room with my mama, and Ray slept in the other room with our daddy. It was a small house, and one built for small aspirations.

Except for mine. "For some reason," my sister says, "you were not like the rest of the family." I never accepted my obvious destiny as a poor-town, don't-accomplish-much housewife. My high school guidance counselor told me to forget about college—"You're not college material, Rita," she said, "just concentrate on finding a good husband and having a family"—but I ignored her advice. (Except for the husband and family part; I did pretty well in *that* department.) It took some doing, but I eventually wormed my way into college and managed to graduate with honors in just three years—and was even president of Kappa Omicron Phi, a society for academic excellence, thank you very much. At that point I got married (there's the husband part), moved out of my childhood home, and more or less began what I suppose you'd call my adult life.

My career as an adult falls pretty much into four parts.

For my first seven years or so after graduating from college, I worked as a teacher, social worker, and consumer service specialist, which is basically someone who helps people understand how to conserve energy and use the stuff they bought.

For the next fifteen years I hosted and produced a national-award-winning daytime television show in Phoenix, Arizona. These were the pre-Oprah, pre–Sally Jesse Raphael, pre–Jerry Springer days; on the national daytime talk scene, Phil Donahue was king. My show was called *Open House*, then *Phoenix at Midday*, *Cooking with Rita*, and finally *The Rita Davenport Show*, which came within a stone's throw of being nationally syndicated. (Close, but no cigar, and I'm grateful it didn't quite happen, because my life would have turned out very differently. More on that later, too.)

By this time I had written a few books that had done pretty well, and also carved out something of a career as a public speaker. The year I finally left the show to speak full-time, I flew however many frequent flier miles around the country it took to give 118 speeches, which works out to almost one every three days.

But I didn't stay in that career, either. Upon leaving the television show I also found myself dabbling in the world of direct selling, becoming an independent representative for a company that sold a line of skin care products. The dabbling got serious, and within six months I was No. 1 in sales and sponsoring. A few years later I was president of that company, a position I held for more than twenty years. When I joined, we were doing close to $4.5 million annually; we soon began experiencing tremendous growth, and two decades later it was just shy of being a billion-dollar company.

Those are the four chapters of my life: teacher and social worker, television host, speaker/author, and company president—although I'll have to admit, as different as those careers sound, it's really been pretty much the same social-worker path the whole time, just in different disguises. I have a passion for helping people, and especially, for helping people discover how great they truly are and what extraordinary riches they have to share with the world. That's my purpose in writing this book, as I'll bet you've already figured out.

I give you my story in a nutshell to make a point: *if I can choose to be successful, then anyone can.*

People sometimes think it's false modesty when I say that. It's not. It's the absolute truth. There have been so many strikes against me, the odds that I should make anything out of myself were just ridiculous.

The other day I went to have my eyes checked. After examining me for a few minutes, the doctor pushed his chair back on its little rolling wheels and said, "Rita, how on earth do you function?"

"What do you mean?"

"Well, you have the weirdest eyesight I ever saw. You use one eye for near vision, and the other one for far vision."

"Is that unusual?" I asked. It sounded pretty normal to me, but hey, what do I know?

He shook his head. "Not by itself, it isn't. But I've never had a patient with this many degrees of difference between their two eyes. I've had one who had three degrees of difference. But you've got *five.*"

I asked him what exactly that meant. He shook his head

again and gave me a look. "When you read something, part of your brain shuts down. And when you're looking out and seeing something in the distance, another part of your brain shuts down. I don't know how you drive, how you park a car, or, frankly, how you do *anything*."

Well, I don't know how I'm doing it either, but apparently it's working for me. I know this: when I'm about to give a speech, I have to take a minute to center myself, so I know exactly what I'm going to say. I go off by myself somewhere backstage, turn up the palms of my hands, and say, "Lord, tell me what you want me to include in my speech today. I know I couldn't do this by myself. There's got to be someone out there who needs a special message. Give me whatever's needed for this group, and I'll do my best to be your messenger." And I'm always grateful when I get the feedback that somehow I said exactly what someone there needed to hear.

When I speak, I tend to go off point and tell stories, and I'm never sure just where they're headed. ("I've noticed," I know, I can hear you saying it.) Most of the time, I do manage to find my way back to where I started and finish making my point, but in the meantime, who knows where we'll wander. It keeps my audiences on edge, wondering, "Okay, is she ever going to finish that thought she started ten minutes ago?"

There's method to the madness, though. It keeps them listening. I learned this from the late great Jack Benny, who was famous for doing this. He could talk to audiences and wander so far off that you'd swear he had no idea what he'd been talking about, when all of a sudden he'd lead right back to the place where he started, almost as if it was by accident. He was brilliant at it.

I interviewed him on my television show many years ago (not long before his death, as it turned out) and I asked him about that. He said, "You know what, Rita, it keeps my audiences more in touch. They think, 'We better keep listening—who knows, maybe the *next* one will make sense.'"

That's how my mind works. It just constantly jumps

from one thought to another. Now that I think about it, I suppose my life has done this too, to some degree. But it's all been in the service of one single-minded goal: to serve as best I could, and do what I was put here to do.

The Music in You

One thing I *don't* want to do is reach the end of my life, face God and say, "Oops. Sorry about that—I know I didn't do that great a job, but you know, it wasn't really what I wanted to be doing anyway…"

How many people trek through life following someone else's script and never get to fly the plane they were supposed to fly? Or spend years wandering off the point but, unlike Jack Benny, never find their way back?

You've no doubt seen the great classic film *It's a Wonderful Life*, where George Bailey thought his life made no difference until, when he was on the verge of suicide, Clarence the angel showed him how much worse off the world would have been without him. As funny a character as that angel is, by the way, has it ever occurred to you why he's called *Clarence*? The name simply means *clarity*. In other words, you have your own angel Clarence, and it's right there inside your head. It's called *clarity about who you are*. How many people commit a slow version of George Bailey's suicide, taking years or decades to let their lives drain away without tapping into the passion of their true purpose?

But if you do touch that purpose and do what you believe in, what you feel passionate about, I can promise you this: you are making a critical difference. There is a greater plan afoot here, and you're part of it.

I'm not a card player, but I have a theory about life and cards. When we're born we're dealt a hand of cards, and each card represents the gift of a talent. You can accept it, love it, and use it, apply it in your life and share it with the world. Or you can abuse it, ignore it, or let it lie fallow. It's your choice.

And you can't reach over and grab my hand of cards,

either, or someone else's hand. No, you've got to play out your own hand. And if you'll take the time to sort through them, you'll find there's at least one ace in there. So find it. And play it.

The people who scream the loudest on their deathbeds are not the ones who regret what they've done. They're the people who regret what they didn't do. I've had quite a few people tell me, "Rita, you do too much." And they may be right. But I would rather wear out than rust out—and I know a lot of people who are rusting out right now. They're dying with their music still in them.

Don't leave this life with your music still in you.

You have a talent. You have a purpose. When you feel good about yourself is when you are using the talents you were given, pursuing the purpose you were put here to fulfill.

Here's what I want you to get from reading this book. I want you to know that if you want it bad enough, the world is *yours*. The world steps aside for the person who knows where they're going. You've got to decide what you want, what you're willing to give up to get it, what your priorities are (in my life it's God first, family second, career third), then get to work doing it—and don't let anyone or anything deter you from your path. I know that sounds simple, and in a way it is. The problem is, we forget it, or it gets drowned out by all the negativity thrown at us. Life circumstances and challenges make it seem complicated. But it really isn't.

There's such sadness and apathy in the world today. So many people don't think there's any chance of making anything great of themselves. But there is not only a chance of it, there is a *certainty*. You can accomplish greatness if you want it bad enough. You have a gift. And when you use it, you *are* a gift.

Before we go on with the rest of this book, I want you to know one more thing: *You are not alone.*

There have been times when I was so frightened, so

out on a limb, so convinced I didn't know what the heck I was doing and there was no way I could get through it all. You may have had experiences where you felt that way too. One day during my first week in television, I was doing an interview (and this was live, not taped), and one of the crew members gave me a signal by crossing his arms in front of his chest. I had no idea what he meant. My first thought was, he was telling me my blouse had come open. Turned out, he was indicating that I had only thirty seconds to finish the segment before we went to a break. I don't remember how I closed that segment, but I do remember this: I was grateful to learn that my blouse was still buttoned.

That same week, I was getting ready to interview the wonderful character actor Eddie Bracken. (You might remember him as Norval Jones, the hero of the Preston Sturges' screwball comedy *The Miracle of Morgan's Creek*—or the sympathetic Walley World theme park founder "Roy Walley" in *National Lampoon's Vacation*.) I was terrified about being around such a celebrity, and in an effort to mollify my nerves by talking about it, I said to Eddie, "You know, I'm always nervous in the beginning of an interview. I just started in television, and I really haven't had any training or much experience. I'm not as nervous once we're both in the camera's eye, 'cause I figure the viewers have already seen me and now they're looking at you—so I kind of relax once we get to a two-shot. But when I'm by myself, I'm nervous as all get-out."

I'll never forget what happened next. We all knew Eddie Bracken as a character—genial, rumpled, scattered, befuddled, hilarious. But this wasn't a movie character. This was the authentic person.

Eddie put his hand on my arm and said, "Rita, don't you know, you are never alone. Do me a favor. Put your fingers on your pulse right here. You feel your pulse? You know what that is? That's the presence of God in you. It's right there, you can feel it. And whenever you wonder where it is, just know this: we are all a part of God. He is always with you."

I'd been going to church my whole life, but I have to tell you, at that moment, my life changed. A kind of calm that I had never experienced came over me.

Now I'm not trying to impose my own spiritual views on you. You believe whatever you believe, and that's the way it should be. I'm not saying you have to believe in the same God I do. That's up to you. My point is just this: *You are not alone.*

You are a child of God, born into this universe a unique part of a world so vast, so limitless, so abundant that it's really quite beyond our comprehension.

I know this: if it were up to me to run the universe, no one would be terribly happy with the results. Hate to break it to you, but the same thing probably goes if it were you running things. That's just not our job, which is perfectly alright, because thankfully the running of the universe is being handled just fine. We don't need to worry about that part. We just need to get down to doing *our* part.

So, just what *is* your part?

Why are you here?

Chapter 2

GREAT EXPECTATION

I like to be on time for important events, but apparently that's been something I've had to learn along the way, because I was about a month late for my own birth.

My older sister Euphiazene and my younger brother Ray both weighed about six pounds at birth. Not me. I kept cooking in the oven for an extra month and emerged weighing eight and a half pounds. My mama said when I was born I already had long fingernails. She also had an explanation for why I was so late being born. "You were up in heaven," she said, "negotiating with God to send you to a wealthy family." She's probably right. One thing's clear: from the very start, for whatever reason, I expected a lot out of life.

I was born Rita Gayle McWhorter. At home, everyone called me Gayle, but something changed on the very first day of first grade. There was a girl in my class named Gail Mangrum, and our teacher, Miss Tyler, said, "We can't have two people with the same name. From now on," she nodded in my direction, "we're going to call you *Rita*, and we're going to call this other little girl *Gail*."

There it was. For the rest of my life, except for the small circle of people who knew me when I was very young, I've been Rita. And the way things worked out in my life, maybe that was no accident. Now, I'm no saint, that's for sure. However, it turns out I have the same name as one. Maybe you know of her. In the opening of the inspirational baseball film *The Rookie*, two nuns are seen praying to Saint Rita to bless the barren land upon which they stand. The idea is that all the amazing and miraculous events that unfold in the course of the rest of the film trace back to the blessing of Saint Rita, who is known as the *patron saint of lost causes and impossible cases.*

In a way, my whole life has been one string of impossible cases, or at least mighty improbable ones, starting with myself.

Actually, starting even before that. When my mama was a young girl herself, according to stories she later told me, there was a witch who lived in the neighborhood. My guess is that today we'd probably call this woman a *psychic* (or maybe a *psychopath*, I'm not sure which), but in any case, in their day she was a witch. One day, this witch got so mad at my mama's grandmother (my great-grandmother) that she put a curse on her and all the women in her family, or so she said. The curse declared that no female in my great-grandmother's family was ever going to succeed —at anything.

My mama told me this story with a curious mix of sardonic amusement and muted reverence. I was only six or so, but I was startled to realize, she *believed* it. I thought it was nonsense. How could someone I'd never even known put a curse on me? I didn't believe a word of it. For my mother, though, I think the story provided a kind of subtle justification not to aspire to much in this life. She was very intelligent, and very strong-minded. In so many ways, she was an amazing woman, and she could have done so much. But she didn't *expect* to—and she set an example for me not to expect much from life either.

My mother never finished high school, even though she

was a very good student, because her family couldn't afford for her to go. They needed her to be working and helping support the family. As a teenager, she went to work as a domestic for another family that was more well off than hers. She never talked about it much, but I could tell she was bitter about it, because she'd liked school and knew she was good at it.

As an adult, my mother did not work outside the home. At one point she was employed briefly at a local hosiery mill, matching up socks. I don't know what happened to that job, but I don't think it lasted more than two weeks. She had no car, and it wouldn't have mattered if she had, because she couldn't drive anyway. Besides, Daddy never encouraged her to work. In fact his position on the matter was this: "If you go to work, I'll quit." He had the macho idea (common in families of that era, at least in our neck of the woods) that if his wife worked, it would send a message that he couldn't provide for his family.

Who needs a witch, when you can put a perfectly fine curse on yourself, just with your own grim expectations?

Where You See Is Where You Go

One day, during that first grade year, I went to visit my aunt's home in College Grove, Tennessee. My grandpa was staying there at the time. Now, I loved my grandpa. (Have you ever noticed how close grandparents are to their grandkids? I'm told that's because they share a common enemy.) I remember sitting with him that evening after dinner on the front porch, me perched on the rough wooden steps, him sitting a few feet away in the rocking chair and smoking his corncob pipe, gray hair, skin all weathered.

My grandpa had worked as a sharecropper all his life, picking cotton and tobacco. He'd worked hard, but not necessarily smart: after all those years, he'd ended up without a penny to live on. This thought was running through my head as we sat, because during the dinner table conversation that evening I'd just heard that he had to go on something called Old Age Assistance (what today we'd call welfare). At the age of six, I wasn't completely sure what that meant, but I could tell by the hushed tone of voice my relatives used and the veiled looks on their faces that it wasn't something anyone was especially proud of.

He didn't seem too concerned, but as I mulled over what I'd heard, I started to worry about him. How come, after all those years of working hard, he now needed to go on Old Age Assistance?

I looked up at him and said, "Grandpa, when you were a young man, where did you think you would end up?"

He didn't answer right away, sat there in his overalls for a moment. I can still hear the creak of that rocking chair on that old wooden porch and smell the tobacco from his corncob pipe.

Finally he said, "You know, Sugar, I s'pose I expected I'd be right where I am. That's one reason I was so glad I had lots of young 'uns. I knew I would always have somewhere to live, and I could go from place to place and have a roof over my head."

He expected to end up in the twilight years of his life having nothing—and that's exactly what happened. It occurred to me that I would end up in life exactly where I saw myself. And I remember thinking, "Boy, that's not where *I'm* headed!"

No one in my family had ever graduated from high school, let alone gone to college. Everyone's expectation was that I would follow suit. Everyone's expectation, that is, except mine. I used to be teased, because I would talk about my future and say that some day I was going to have a house that would make Scarlett O'Hara's mansion Tara from *Gone with the Wind* look like a tract house, and I was going to have a fancy new car, and I was going to travel ... and Momma would say, "What makes you think those things?! Where do you get those wild ideas? Don't you go getting your hopes up!"

Don't get your hopes up... I always thought that was the most ridiculous thing to say. What kind of sense does *that* make? I mean, what good are low hopes? No, I think high hopes are the only kind worth having. And high expectations are even better. A hope says, "I'd *like* to do that." An expectation says, "I *will* do that."

In the last chapter I pointed out that when you are hot with enthusiasm for what you're doing, you become magnetized and start attracting the people, resources, and circumstances that you need to fulfill whatever dream it is you're pursuing. Now I want to describe the mechanism through which that happens, and it comes down to one word: *expectation*. What you expect, believe, or picture is what you get—no more, no less.

It isn't enough just to want something. In order to achieve it, create it, attract it, build it, you have to not only want that thing, but also create in your mind a crystal clear image of what it is you want. Remember Clarence the angel? Exercising that clarity around your purpose, your dreams, and your passionate pursuit is what creates an image vivid and tangible enough that it becomes real, and not only to you, but also to others. When you paint a picture of something that is so clear that you can see it vividly, that it starts to become real in your mind, then here's what happens: you start to *expect* it.

There's a world of difference between hope and expectation. A hope is a vague wish, a fuzzy sense of something you want but can't quite see, because it isn't quite real. When it becomes as clear as glass, then it's not a hope—it's an expectation.

A hope is something that *might* happen. An expectation is something that *will* happen. Confidence rises when you act as if what you expect has already happened.

My mama had a good point, though: Where *did* I get those wild ideas? I'll tell you where: I was born with them, and so were you. *Everyone* starts out with big dreams. Remember the sperm-swimming Olympics?

That time Dolly Parton visited Phoenix and appeared as a guest on my show, she talked about the circumstances of her childhood.

Dolly was raised in the hills of Sevierville, Tennessee,

about an hour's drive west of where I grew up. Her family was so poor they may have been even poorer than we were: she described growing up in a dilapidated old one-room cabin. She told me about the story behind her hit song, "Coat of Many Colors," which describes how her mother took rags that had been given to the family and sewed them together to make her a coat. She was so proud of that coat. (I didn't mention it at the time, but as she described it to me, I couldn't help thinking of my *theed thack* dress.)

"Dolly," I asked her, "did you ever expect to be rich and famous?"

Now in the course of fifteen years of television I've asked that question to an awful lot of celebrities. Sometimes the person will get all humble and aw-shucks on me, kind of bow their head a little and say, "Oh my, no, I never had any idea. I've been so fortunate, and who could have ever imagined that all this would happen, blah blah blah..."

I loved Dolly's answer.

"Heck, yeah! Rita, I always knew that I was going to be exactly where I am today. My poverty was just a minor inconvenience at the time."

You show me a millionaire who says he made his millions by accident, a movie star or recording icon who says her only ambition was ever to wait tables, without a thought of fame and fortune, and who ended up at the top through a string of coincidences and lucky breaks that had nothing to do with her, really ... and I'll show you a liar of epic proportion. Folks, if it happened, they first *expected* it!

Everything and everyone starts out with a dream. Too many of us put our dreams in our back pockets when circumstances start beating us up, and then forget we put them there and never take them out again. After a while of being beaten up by circumstances, we start beating ourselves up too.

Here's the thing: *It costs you nothing to dream—but everything if you don't.*

Einstein once said, "Imagination is more important than intelligence." And that's coming from someone who had more than a little intelligence. I think he had it exactly right, too, because it takes imagination to dream, and a powerful dream trumps intelligence or any other attribute or strength anytime. I'd add this, though: imagination *with conviction* is more important than intelligence.

Raise your expectations. Dream big! Aim for the moon; you might not hit it, but if you miss you're bound to hit a star.

The Expectations of Others

Our home in Flat Rock happened to be located just 100 yards shy of the minimum distance from Turner School that would qualify us to go on the school bus, so we had to walk to school, even in the snow and rain. Sometimes, though, Daddy would drive us, along with a carload of neighborhood kids.

He worked two jobs, six and a half days a week, to provide for his family, making minimum wage—if that. At night he worked at a gas station, mostly for tips. He was a good man and a wonderful father, and he always treated us kids well. But he spoke two languages: English and Profanity. When he got behind the wheel, he seemed to feel it was his moral obligation to cuss out every other driver on the road. (This was usually after he and Mama had verbally tangled; I suppose today we'd call it *road rage*.) He'd vent his frustration at everyone else, right out there in front of God, his children and everyone in earshot. It was embarrassing.

At the same time, I have to admit, it was also educational. I picked up a lot of colorful turns of phrase and learned something that has served me well the rest of my life: *language can be a lot of fun*. (Also, sometimes it's important to know what *not* to say.)

Often the assignment we're given in life appears as a challenge, even an insurmountable one. Mine was to be a speaker, trainer, and motivator—and lo and behold, as I mentioned earlier, I was born with a speech impediment. Hey, at least I was in good company. I'm told that Moses had a speech impediment, too, and when God told him to get off his rear end and do what he was supposed to do, he kind of dug his heels and gave God a little pushback. "Hey, I really can't talk that well, you think maybe we'd be better off if we, you know, got my brother Aaron to do that part?..." (I know what you're thinking: "Wait a minute. Did she really just compare herself to *Moses*?" Well yes, I suppose I did, but not to his more complimentary aspects.)

At Turner School, they thought I should be put into Special Education because of my speech impediment. Back then Special Ed was pretty much for kids who were severely handicapped or profoundly learning-disabled (although that was not the term they used in those days, and in no way were these kids ever given the opportunity to be "mainstream"). What they were really saying was that they didn't see much hope for me, and they would rather shuffle me to the back of the bus where I wouldn't interfere with the education of normal kids. Now *that* is low expectations.

Before that could happen, though, we took an unexpected trip. A few weeks later my mother's sister, who lived all the way out in California, became gravely ill with breast cancer. My mother packed up my brother and me and the three of us traveled together by train out to the West Coast to see her. For a six-year-old who'd never been outside her little sphere, traveling cross-country by train from Tennessee to California was an incredible experience. We stayed in California for almost two months, helping take care of my aunt.

Soon after we arrived, Mother enrolled me in the first grade in a school there in California. A few days later, she got a call from the principal's office. "We have tested your daughter Rita," they said, "and we want to discuss the results with you."

Mother said, "Well, I think I know what you're going to say...." Of course, she figured they were going to tell her that they also recommended putting me into Special Ed.

"Oh, good," they said, "we're glad this comes as no surprise. Well, Mrs. McWhorter, from our testing we see that your daughter is gifted, and we want to move her from the first grade to the third grade."

My mother waited for a moment, sure she had heard

them wrong. Then she cleared her throat and said, "'Scuse me?" They repeated their message. I'm not sure she ever fully heard what they said. I can't imagine how they managed to terminate the conversation.

So there it was: I traveled two thousand miles by rail and in the process went from being "special needs" to being "gifted." I'm not entirely sure what that says about the California school system, but then, who am I to judge?

But the truly amazing thing about it was what happened when I got back home two months later and went back into the first grade with Miss Tyler.

"Miss Tyler, I'm back," I said my first day back in the classroom, "and guess what? I'm *gifted!*"

I walked like a gifted child, talked like a gifted child, and performed like a gifted child. I said, "Miss Tyler, I'd like to help out with some of the slower students, if that's okay." And I did. I went around the classroom and helped some of the other kids with their schoolwork, and even helped them put their coats and sweaters on.

If I was fortunate enough to be gifted, then it made sense that I ought to share whatever those gifts were with the people around me, right? And you know, even though I'm not six years old anymore, that still seems to me like a philosophy that makes sense.

Many years later, I had the chance to visit Miss Tyler on her ninety-ninth birthday and thank her for all she did for me. She remembered that time well and said she had never seen such a transformation. "I'll never forget how profoundly you changed," she told me. "You suddenly became my little assistant, because you believed with all your heart that you were gifted. As a first grader, you even wrote an illustrated poem about Easter that was published in the school paper!"

What really happened here? I mean, was I really gifted? Of course I was—we *all* are; but it wasn't like I suddenly had any special abilities or qualities that I hadn't already had before. No, that wasn't what changed. What changed was *how I saw myself.*

Contagious Expectations

What happened to me in first grade is far from unique. It happens to us all the time. In psychology and management circles, it's called the Pygmalion Effect: the self-fulfilling prophecy. Another term for it is the Rosenthal Effect, named after Harvard professor Robert Rosenthal, who conducted a famous study in the 1960s. In Rosenthal's "Oak School experiment," elementary school teachers were told that certain first-grade through fifth-grade students had higher IQs and were likely to exhibit more intellectual growth and development than the other students.[5] There wasn't a lick of truth to it—the students had been chosen randomly. But the teachers didn't know that.

Sure enough, when the children were all tested at the end of the school year, those students' IQs had gone up significantly and they had all performed far better than their peers. To put it simply, they rose to the level of their teachers' expectations—even though those expectations had absolutely no basis in any objective reality.

And in case you're thinking, "Oh well, first-graders, that's not surprising, they're so impressionable and malleable when they're so young," here's something that might interest you: according to Professor Rosenthal, further studies with college and graduate students have shown that *the exact same thing happens with adults, too*.[6] Yes, expectations really are that powerful.

Those teachers' expectations were contagious. Even though they were unspoken, and the teachers didn't mean to give any outward indication that they were treating certain students any differently from the others, they couldn't help it, because expectations are so powerful you can't hide them. Like catching a cold from a sneeze, those kids caught their teachers' expectations and started seeing themselves differently. Because the teachers expected more from them, they began expecting more from themselves—just the way I did after being put into the "gifted" program in California.

According to the Rolling Stones, you can't always get

what you want, and while I'm not saying Mick Jagger is the world's most astute philosopher, in my observation that's quite true. But I'll tell you what you *will* get: exactly what you expect. Look around you, at the life you have today. You know what that is you're seeing? The result of your expectations, no more and no less.

What are your own expectations? You'd better get clear on them, because if you don't expect much, you're not going to get much. On the other hand, if you expect greatness, then greatness is what you'll have in your life.

Two Ears and One Crown

By the time I was in the sixth grade, I had about *half* figured this out.

At Turner School we had an annual contest to help generate funds to support the school's upkeep. That September, as classes were under way, we all started getting ourselves organized in an effort to collect pennies to help buy new playground equipment. We knew that at the end of the contest, when the collections were all tallied by school officials, the class who had gathered the most pennies would win. What's more—and this was the kicker—the boy and girl who had spearheaded that class's effort would be named King and Queen of the school.

I was only eleven, but I wanted to win that crown. I'm told that middle children are often overachievers because they want so badly to succeed at something. I confess: in this regard, I was the classic middle child.

I managed to get myself voted sixth grade representative and right away started rallying my troops. "We have got to win this to show the rest of the school what we're made of," I told my classmates. "Our honor is at stake here!" You'd have thought we were the three hundred Spartans going up against Xerxes and all his thousands of troops in a battle to the death. My old friend and classmate Mary Kathryn Craig remembers this well, and tells me I convinced everyone that we had the best class in the whole school, we had the best students, we had the best teachers, and if we worked the hardest, and we could raise more pennies than anyone. There were about thirty kids in that class, and I remember being determined that my great expectation was going to rub off on every one of them.

One day Miss Elliot, who lived across the street from us, happened to be visiting at our house, and I mentioned to her that I was going to win this contest over at Turner School.

Miss Elliot was one of the few women on Raymond Street who worked. Most of the women in our neighborhood were just like my mother: they had no car (and couldn't drive anyway), no education, and no job opportunities. But Miss Elliot had moved from some other state and had come from a different background, and she had a job selling clothing at a dry goods store. She also happened to be president of the PTA.

"Oh no," she said, "you're not going to win that. You're wasting your time and all your classmates' time. Here's what will happen: Some daddy in the school who has money is going to make a donation to the school. He'll write a check, and his little girl will win the contest. That's the way it happens every year. I'm sorry, but you have no chance."

I stuck up for myself. "Nuh-uh," I said. "I'm going to win."

She shook her head and said, "You're just getting your hopes up."

Sheesh, there was that business with the low hopes again. What was it with these grownups, anyway?

Miss Elliot glanced at me, and then peered closer. I was wearing my hair in a pony tail, as I normally did, and I realized she was looking at my ears.

"Goodness, child, look at this," she said. "One of your ears is a bit lower than the other. And one seems to stick out more than the other."

Now I had never noticed this. If there was a difference between my two ears, it was so slight that I'd never seen it, and neither had anyone else, as far as I knew. In fact, when I study my reflection in the mirror even today, I still can't see it. But Miss Elliot's offhand comment made me so self-conscious about my ears that I stopped wearing my hair in a pony tail.

It's amazing how easily we turn our own power over to other people, and give them the ability to make us feel bad about ourselves.

Which is why I say I had *half*-learned about the power of expectation. I didn't yet have the self-sufficiency it would have taken to shake off her observation and keep proudly wearing my pony tail. But while she may have gotten to me in terms of my appearance, she was *not* going to take away my dream.

"I'm going to have to work harder," I thought. "That's all." And I did.

My mother used to say, "Gayle, you are the most bull-headed kid I've ever seen." I'm sure she was not exaggerating about that. But if you're the parent of a bull-headed kid, let me tell you something: that is not necessarily a negative thing. Many years later, a teacher from my school days heard me give a speech at a ceremony where I was being given an award. I had no idea she was in the audience and didn't recognize her until she came right to me afterward to greet me. "You know," she said, "I've been following your career, and I've tried to figure out how you've done all the things you've done. Because honestly, you were never that academically gifted."

I laughed and thanked her for that candid assessment, then waited to see what else she had to say.

"Well," she went on, "today I figured it out. You were always so bull-headed that when people told you that you couldn't do something, you just didn't listen. You expected to do it anyway."

Which brings us back to sixth grade.

I don't know if there were any well-to-do daddies who wrote donation checks that year, but if there were, it didn't do any good as far as that contest was concerned. Our class raised about eight hundred dollars, which was a lot of money in those days, and I was crowned Queen of Turner School.

I'll never forget the look on Miss Elliot's face when I

came up on stage to where she stood and she put that crown on my head, ears and all. She may have been trying to hide it, but I could tell she was shocked. I looked up at her, smiled, and winked.

A Vote of Confidence

In the eighth grade I had a teacher named Miss Ruth Quarles. We referred to her in whispers as an *old maid*; in reality, she was probably no more than thirty-five years old, but she was single and she was tough, a really strict disciplinarian, and had a reputation of expecting a *lot* from her students. When you were in Miss Quarles's class, you kept on your toes. And I'll have to give her this, too: when you left her class, you really had learned your stuff.

At this point I was captain of the cheerleaders' squad, something I was completely thrilled about and devoted to. I stood at less than five feet and weighed less than a hundred pounds soaking wet—but I had the loudest cheer in Davidson County. They called me the Mouth of the South. It's a miracle I didn't ruin my vocal chords. We were very animated and energetic; we had practiced all summer, and we were good.

Mama had already told me I couldn't be a cheerleader, because we couldn't afford a new cheerleading outfit, so over the summer I baby-sat and cleaned houses and managed to earn the eight dollars it cost to purchase a used outfit. I bought it from someone who was about six inches taller than me, so I had to roll up the waist around my middle like big donut. It's a wonder the thing didn't fall off me when we were jumping around.

It was September, and we had our first pep rally coming up. There would be at least 800 kids there in the gymnasium, and I would be the one leading the whole thing. This was too exciting for words!

Two days before the pep rally, Miss Quarles did not show up for school. It was hard to imagine her being sick; she seemed invincible and impervious to the vicissitudes of ordinary life. (Colds and flu? Miss Quarles? Impossible!)

But for whatever reason, she was out for two days, and instead we had a substitute teacher who gave us an assignment to diagram ten sentences. Well, nobody paid any attention to substitute teachers, right? I mean, as far as we could see, they were really essentially just baby-sitters. I never dreamed that Miss Quarles would actually ask for that homework assignment. So I did two of the ten sentences, and figured I was home free. In other words, I blew it off.

The day of the pep rally Miss Quarles returned to class— and sure enough, she asked for the homework. I turned in my two sentences. After she'd collected all our papers and taken a minute to leaf through them, she looked up. "Now, some of you didn't finish," she said. Then she turned her gaze to me. "Rita, why didn't you do ten sentences?"

"Oh, well, Miss Quarles," I said, turning on my maximum thirteen-year-old charm, "that teacher just wasn't as good as you are at explaining things, and, well, I just didn't understand it."

Of course I was lying through my teeth.

She looked at me. "Fine," she said. Then she asked the same question to all the other kids who hadn't finished the assignment, one by one, and they all repeated some version of the same thing I'd said.

"All right then," she pronounced. "For all of you children who didn't understand how to diagram the sentences, you will stay in during the pep rally, and I will help you finish that assignment."

There was a moment of silence as we all processed what she had just said. I think we had studied something about English history, about how Henry the Eighth had had all these different wives, and how it seemed like they all ended up having their heads chopped off. We had also studied about the French Revolution. In that moment of silence, I thought I heard the sound of the guillotine's blade falling on Marie Antoinette's dainty neck, the sound of the executioner's axe silencing Anne Boleyn's eloquence forever. It was a long moment. Was she really going to keep us in? It wasn't possible—I mean, there I was, with my eight-dollar cheerleader's outfit on, donut waist and all!

Then the moment was over, and class continued on as if nothing had happened. This was real. She wasn't kidding.

Lunchtime came, and I sat at a table in the cafeteria eating a bowl of chili with tears running down my cheeks and dropping into the bowl. I felt so sorry for myself, and so did my friends and peers, who circled around to sympathize. Misery loves company.

After lunch I went up to her as contrite and serious as I could be and said, in a low confidential tone, "Miss Quarles, may I talk to you for a second?"

"Yes, Rita?" she said.

"Miss Quarles," I said. "I'm the captain of the cheerleaders' team. I *have* to be there! This is *important*."

She looked at me, very calm, and said, "I'm sorry, Rita, but you need to get your homework done."

"You *witch!*" was what I thought to myself. But what I said was, "I could stay after school and do it. Or I could come in early tomorrow morning."

She just shook her head. She was firm about it. There wasn't anything that was going to change her mind: I was staying in during the rally and finishing that homework.

There were about eight of us who remained in the classroom the entire time that pep rally went on, as scheduled. Our classroom was close enough to the gymnasium that we could hear every single thing that happened in there, and pretty soon we heard kids starting to stomp their feet in rhythm and chant, *"We want Ri-ta! We want Ri-ta!"* I felt I was about to burst into tears, but somehow I managed to keep my game face on. I walked up through the aisle of desks to the blackboard and started diagramming those sentences.

It was one of the longest hours I've ever experienced. I still remember the distant sounds of chanting, cheering, stomping, and whistles, wafting in like fragmentary messages from another universe, and the hushed stillness of our classroom, broken only by the slow, studious scrape and squeak of our chalk on the board.

When the pep rally was over, the kids all came bustling noisily back into the classroom and took their seats. Miss Quarles waited until the room quieted down, and then she spoke.

"I want to say something. This was a very challenging pep rally, because the captain of the cheerleaders, Rita McWhorter, had to stay in and complete the homework she hadn't done."

The room was utterly silent now, except for the pounding of my own pulse in my ears.

"Now, I want to make a prediction," Miss Quarles continued. "Through this all, Rita had the best attitude. She was courteous, friendly, and cooperative. She didn't seem bitter or angry. She handled the situation in a very mature way. My prediction is this: If she can handle adversity that well, at this stage in her life, Rita McWhorter will make something of herself someday."

I'll be honest, that last part felt like it pretty much went right over my head at the time. But on some level, it stuck with me. *Rita McWhorter will make something of herself someday.*

Fifty years later I was able to find Miss Quarles, and I sent her flowers on her birthday and called to thank her for being such a good teacher, and for her encouragement. I wished I'd done it earlier, and regret not having gotten back in touch with more of my teachers to tell them how much I appreciated them. (I can't recommend this practice strongly enough. You might want to give it a try; I can promise it will be a rewarding experience—for both of you.)

One of the greatest gifts you can give another human being—whether it is a student, a colleague, your spouse or child, or even someone you've just met and may know for only a short time—is your own great expectation for their future. Behind every great achievement, every success, every realized dream, there is at least one person who saw it happening *before* it happened.

I was always grateful for the "meanest teacher in the school," who turned out not to be so mean after all … and who showed me the power of great expectation.

Chapter 3

GRATITUDE

When I was sixteen, I was nominated by the junior class to be one of our candidates for that year's high school Band Queen.

This was quite an honor. Every year, there was a concert put on by the band department of the school. During the concert the candidates, two nominated from each class, would parade around the gymnasium in their evening gowns, just like a Miss America contest, and everyone in attendance would have the opportunity to cast a ballot. The winner would be that year's Band Queen.

I didn't just want to win this; I wanted to win it *bad*. It seems such a small thing now, but at the time, it meant so much. I suppose it was that middle child thing again: maybe what it was I so desperately wanted was the social acknowledgment. Maybe it was the sense of achievement. In any case, whatever the underlying reason, I *wanted* it.

However, I didn't have the evening dress I needed to compete in the Band Queen contest, and as with my cheerleader outfit in sixth grade, there was no way we could afford to buy one—and this time earning baby-sitting money to buy a used one wasn't going to work.

Fortunately for me, I had a friend named Judy Boyd. Her mother was a teacher and her daddy had a good job, and Judy always wore the nicest clothes. What's more, she knew the number one seamstress in Nashville. Judy graciously agreed to loan me an exquisite evening dress that I knew couldn't help but earn everyone's admiration. Now I was all set. Band Queen was in my sights!

Soon after Judy had loaned me the dress, I was walking home from school one day and as I got closer to home, I thought I smelled something in the air. Something like smoke. I came to our block—and there were two fire trucks parked there on my street. They were parked, in fact, right in front of my home.

We had been having our floors sanded and varnished that day. Apparently the man who was putting on the final coat of varnish had lit a cigarette, and the varnish had caught fire.

I've mentioned that we lived in a little house with two bedrooms; Momma and I slept in twin beds in one room, and Daddy and Ray slept in twin beds in the other room. In our room, Momma and I shared a tiny closet, and she used to say, "Gayle, you've got a whole closet full of clothes!" the joke being that this meant I had next to nothing. Only now it was no joke: I really did have nothing. That fire had burned up about half the house, including our living room and Momma's and my bedroom, along with everything in it. The only thing I had left was the dress on my back—and it wasn't my favorite.

I hadn't owned much stuff, but it was *my* stuff. And now all my worldly possessions had been reduced to a wet, smoking mound of rubble. I felt heartsick, angry, and resentful.

But here's the funny thing: with each passing year, I feel more and more grateful that this happened. How can you truly appreciate everything you have until you know what it's like not to have anything at all?

The Gift of Poverty

I've mentioned that we were poor, but I haven't really explained how important that poverty was to me.

"Why," you may ask, "in a book on creating a rich, successful life, are you talking about poverty like it's some great thing? I don't need to hear about poverty—I already know how to do that just fine!"

Maybe so, but if you're going to create a rich life, you have to know where you're starting from. If you ask me, "How do I get to Phoenix?" I can't tell you—not yet. Not until I know where you're starting from. It's worth taking a good look at poverty, because if you don't know what being poor is, how can you ever truly know what it means to be wealthy?

I sure didn't see it that way at the time, but I now believe growing up in poverty was the greatest gift in my life. If we hadn't been so poor, I would never have had the work ethic and street smarts it took to succeed—or the desire. I wouldn't have had the *hunger*.

I'm not saying it's better to be poor, and I'm certainly not saying that the kind of starvation and genuine suffering so many millions of children around the globe experience still today isn't a terrible thing. It is a travesty and deserves every ounce of our effort and energy to change. I'm talking about the kind of poverty I experienced growing up, where the basic needs of living were covered—the security of a roof overhead and food on the table—but there was little else beyond that.

What I'm saying is, the circumstances in our lives that look like the greatest hardships often turn out to have the greatest blessings tucked secretly inside. And the same thing goes for those circumstances that look like great fortune. It's easy for the trappings of success to spoil you—unless you truly know how to appreciate them.

For example, looking back I realize that we ate very little meat when I was growing up. We had beef or pork maybe once a week, and chicken once a week, but most of the time it was just vegetables. In fact, here's something ironic:

throughout history, at least until recently, the poor often ate a much healthier diet than the very rich. For centuries and centuries, it was people in the wealthiest classes who suffered from diabetes, heart disease, and obesity. (Now *that's* something to think about. Having a rich life and being materially rich are not necessarily the same thing.)

Like all types of adversity, poverty is a gateway to the most powerful success secret I know of: gratitude. Being grateful isn't just a nice way to be. Yes, writing thank-you notes is a good thing to do. But it's more than a matter of being "nice" or "a good person." Gratitude is *powerful*. It changes you. Gratitude may well be the most direct pathway there is to genuine prosperity.

In all the great religions around the world and down through history, there are two main types of prayer. There is the *prayer of petition*: asking for what you want. "Lord," sang Janis Joplin, "won't you buy me a Mercedes-Benz?" And then there is the *prayer of appreciation*: thanking God for what you've already been given. Prayers are prayers, and they're all good—but as far as I'm concerned, that second kind is far more powerful.

Gratitude is like expectation. When you are grateful for something, it magnetizes you. You attract more of that which you're grateful for, because you always attract more of what you focus on. The world reacts creatively to our images of thought. What you think about, you bring about.

You're probably wondering what happened to Judy Boyd's evening dress. As it happened, the day before the fire, when I heard that our floors were going to be sanded the next day, I took that dress out of our closet and brought it over to a neighbor's house across the street for safe-keeping, so it wouldn't get any sawdust on it. It was the only thing I had, other than the clothes on my back, that survived the fire.

There's more to the story of Judy Boyd's dress and the Band Queen contest, too … but we'll get there in a little bit.

The Sting of Prejudice

That same year, when I was sixteen, I went to work at

Woolworth's. There was a water fountain with a sign over it that said, White, and another water fountain with a sign that said, colored. This was the late fifties, and segregation was alive and well in the South. It drove me crazy. Every day I would ride the bus downtown to work, and there would always be "colored" people sitting in a knot in the back of the bus. The first time I saw it I thought, "What on Earth is *this* all about?!" Every day, I would get on the bus, walk back there, and sit with them out of rebellion.

When I was a toddler my mother went through a fairly long period of being quite sick. A friend of ours knew a woman who was available to help out, and she started coming in and baby-sitting for my sister and me. I have no idea how we were able to afford her services; she probably worked for very little pay, and perhaps meals. All I know is that she was African American, her name was Hattie, and I adored her. I have no clear memories of Hattie, but years later my mother told me about those times, how I would kiss her and say I wanted to go home with her. "Oh, Gayle," she told me, "you were crazy about her." After reading Kathryn Stockett's novel *The Help* and watching the film version, I have the feeling that Hattie was telling me, "You is kind, you is smart, you is important."

I don't know if it was because of my time with Hattie, or just because of who I was, but I could never understand why people would discriminate against others because of the color of their skin. I had enough consciousness even back then to know that we were all human beings, all God's children.

And it wasn't just about color.

Every one of us has at some point felt the sting of prejudice or rejection, of being made to feel inferior to others, of being treated unfairly by life. For me, it wasn't about being black or white, it was about being poor. My family's poverty always made me feel inferior to others of my age group. But you can be white and well off and still feel inferior to others. Some people are slower than others; some people are discriminated against because they're too smart. You could be too short, too tall, too fat, too skinny. Or have the wrong accent.

Decades later, when I was working full-time as a speaker, I was invited to give a talk to 1,800 college professors in Yonkers, New York. The night before the presentation, I got a call at my hotel room from the woman who was hosting me there, just to touch base and make sure all our arrangements were set.

We had never talked on the phone before, and evidently, she had never heard me speak. After we'd been talking a few minutes, she said, "Um, excuse me, but do you ... do you always speak *Southern*?"

Well, what could I say? "Yes, Dr. Hostess." (Her name was not really Hostess, of course, but she did have a Ph.D.) "I was raised in the South, and as a result, yes, I do have a Southern accent."

"Ah," she said. There was a brief pause, and then she added, "You don't *look* Southern in your pictures."

A flash of images went through my mind: what did it look like to *look Southern*?

"Well, Dr. Hostess," I said, "if you're worried about it, I want to assure you of one thing: I *will* be wearing shoes on stage tomorrow."

I'm not sure if she thought that wasn't funny or was just too distracted by her concerns to get the humor of it. "Well, here's the thing," she said. "We have you scheduled for an hour and a half, but I'm wondering, under the circumstances, would you do me a favor? Could you cut it down to, say, forty minutes?"

I said, "Dr. Hostess, I flew six hours to get here, but I'll be happy to speak for forty minutes, if that's all you want."

The next day, I spoke for forty minutes—and when I finished the 1,800 college professors gave me a long standing ovation. I looked over at Dr. Hostess, who had approached me from the wings to introduce the next speaker, smiled and said, as I departed the stage, "It's that Southern accent. Don't they just love it?"

I've learned that every successful person, at some time

in their life, has felt subjected to prejudice or felt inferior. It's what you do to overcome that feeling that makes all the difference.

Appreciation

In the years right after high school I encountered the work of William James, the father of modern psychology, and it was when reading James that I first found a way to put what I was learning into words.

In 1896 a class of his at Radcliffe College sent James a potted azalea, which so touched him that he penned a thank-you letter to the class, and in it he wrote that he had just realized he had left "one immense omission" in his writings on psychology:

> The deepest principle of Human Nature is the
> *craving to be appreciated.*[7]

I remember feeling electrified the first time I read those words. This insight has since come to serve as a cornerstone of my life: to love what is and find the good in everybody. It's so easy to focus on the worst in people. It's far more powerful to keep your eye out for the best in people, and always strive to see others in terms of their highest and greatest potential.

Ken Blanchard and Spencer Johnson made this idea famous thirty years ago with *The One Minute Manager*, still one of the most popular business management books of all time. One of the secrets to raising productivity levels in any organization, say Blanchard and Johnson, is to *catch people doing things right* and to praise them for it, on the spot and publicly. In fact, if you want a powerful secret to increasing other people's productivity, here it is: *Praise in public, criticize in private.* Provide people with a high-morale-producing environment, and they will generally rise to your expectations.

In the book *Go-Givers Sell More*, my coauthor John David Mann and his coauthor Bob Burg say this:

> The word *appreciate* comes from the Latin
> *appretiare*, which means "to set a price to."
> Over the centuries it came to mean both "an
> expression of one's estimate of something,
> usually favorable" and "to rise in value."
> Interesting: when you appreciate people, *you*
> appreciate. And when you don't, you *depreciate*.
> You want to increase your own worth?
> *Appreciate.*[8]

The more you appreciate people, the more you *appreciate*—the more valuable you become. And the world will reward you for being valuable.

Put Your Best into Use

I was once on an airplane that happened to run smack into a freak weather pattern and suddenly dropped ten thousand feet in a matter of seconds. Everyone was screaming, food trays were flying in the air, and the cabin was drenched in panic and adrenaline. We were all about to die, and we all knew it.

And what went through my mind in those several brief seconds, as I faced my own certain demise? "I am so grateful that all my lingerie matches. When they pull my body out of the wreckage, at least I'm going to look good." I also noted with satisfaction that my hair was clean.

And then something else flashed through my mind: my good crystal.

When we were kids, Mama used to save the jars that fruit preserves came in, wash them out, and use them for drinking glasses. I have vivid memories of drinking juice and milk in washed-out fruit jars. I don't remember when or how I first became aware that there was such a thing in the world as Waterford crystal, but ever since I had badly wanted to have a set of my very own. Early in my adult life, when I was working multiple jobs and barely scraping by, I started buying myself a few really nice things, one piece at a time. A tiny silver teaspoon; a little fine china teacup and saucer. One summer, when I was working as a teacher, I took an additional job and with the extra money, I finally went out and bought myself a set of Waterford crystal glassware. I rarely used these things; I just kept them in a cupboard "for nice."

And now, decades later as I sat in that plummeting airplane with people screaming around me, I realized I had entire sets of beautiful china, silver, and crystal at home, sitting on shelves in cupboards, hardly ever used because I had been saving them all for "special occasions," and worried they might get chipped or cracked.

I hadn't been using what I had. I hadn't been truly *appreciating* what I had. Now *that* gave me something I would have to think about later—if there were going to be any later.

I heard a voice in my head ask, "Rita, do you think Second Wife will worry about chipping that good china?"

Oh, Lord. I knew the answer to that one.

Of course, I didn't die that day after all. None of us did. The weather anomaly passed, the pilot got control, and we all reached terra firma just fine. When I got home, I took out one of those crystal glasses and made myself a nice tall drink of cold delicious iced tea.

Do you have any idea how good iced tea tastes in Waterford crystal?

Since then, I've used my china, crystal, and silver every single day I've been in my home—because *life* is a special occasion. And besides, if anyone deserves to chip that china, it's me, because I bought it. I think I'll have to give it all away, though, while I'm still alive. Unless their wives value china, crystal, and silver, my kids will be tempted to hold a garage sale adjacent to my funeral.

Do you have good china, crystal, or silverware that you never use, because you're saving it "for special"? And what about the finest aspects of *you*?

We all have God-given abilities and talents, and just like precious china and crystal, they're not doing anyone any good stored away in cupboards waiting for a special occasion. The same is true of your dreams. When I exhort you to grab hold of your dreams with all the passion you can muster and throw yourself headlong into their pursuit, I'm not saying that purely for your benefit. Yes, I want you to gain the fulfillment from them that you deserve. But it's also for the sake of others. Think of how many people whose lives you will positively affect in the course of realizing your fondest aspirations—and whose lives you'll be cheating if you draw back and never engage.

Pursuing your greatest potential is not only an act of ambition, but also an expression of gratitude and appreciation. It means being grateful for the gifts you have been given, by giving them full expression, and not squirreling them away on a shelf where they'll never see the light of day. If you're not *using* the best in yourself, you're not *appreciating* the best in yourself. Which means you're *depreciating*.

Yes, it's powerful to dream about the future, but you can't live in the future. It's also powerful to learn from the past, but you can't live there either. (If you try, it'll only make you senile.) The only place you have to live in is right now.

When you are grateful for what you have, right here and right now, you become like a magnet and attract to yourself even greater opportunities, gifts, and benefits. Gratitude is the most important step in achievement and prosperity. Be grateful for what you've got, and more will come to you. The past is a canceled check; the future is a promissory note; the only real legal tender is this moment, right now. Make the most of today.

Buried Treasure

Do you have any problems? Of course you do. So do I. We've all got problems. I'm going to show you a way to get rid of your problems. It's a game that has only two rules, and it goes like this:

The first rule of the game is that you can get rid of your problem simply by bringing it over to me and setting it down, right here in front of me. Then I blow a whistle, and someone else comes over, picks your problem up, and carts it away.

Isn't that easy? Isn't that great?

But here's the second rule: when I blow the whistle, you also have to pick up somebody else's problem and cart *it* away—and you don't get to choose which one.

Hmm. Puts things in a different perspective, doesn't it?

I once interviewed a couple on my television show who had a beautiful six-month-old baby girl, only they had never laid eyes on her—because they were both blind from birth. Do you have any idea what they would pay you for your eyes, just to see their baby for five minutes?

Another time, I interviewed a woman who had been born without any arms. She had learned to put her contact lens in with her toes. I was flabbergasted—I would think putting those things in with your fingers would be hard enough. Can you imagine what she would pay you for your arms, just to hold her baby when she nursed it, or to be able to give someone a hug? How often do we refrain from giving someone else a hug, and us with two good working arms? I can promise you this: if that woman suddenly had your arms, she would be a person who was very generous with hugs.

On one show I interviewed a man who had pursued a career as a professional golfer. He'd worked three years to get his PGA (Professional Golfers Association) card. It was a proud day, he told me, and he'd never forget the feeling of holding that card in his hand. The following day he was in an automobile accident that left him a paraplegic.

"You know what I'd give to have someone else's legs," he told me, "just for a day? Heck, just for an hour—long enough to shoot nine holes in the rain?"

One of my dearest friends was the bestselling writer and humorist Erma Bombeck, who lived on top of a mountain in the same neighborhood as my husband and me. (I used to say, "I live a few million dollars down from Erma Bombeck.") In the mid-nineties, for her last book, Erma received a $14 million advance. When I heard that I was in awe and so proud for her. Imagine: $14 million, before she'd even written a word. I asked her, "Erma, what does it feel like to get a $14 million advance?"

She looked at me and said, "You know, Rita, I'd rather have a kidney."

Erma was diagnosed with polycystic kidney disease when she was only twenty years old. Although she managed to keep it private and people by and large didn't know about it, she was plagued with terrible health problems her whole life. I often wonder: if she had not seen such suffering herself, would she have been able to write the words that brought so much joy and laughter to millions of people? At the time of this $14 million conversation, Erma was on dialysis three days a week. She would eventually have a kidney transplant and die from complications following the surgery.

As you're reading this, I'd like you to do something: reach around behind yourself with one hand and place your palm over the small of your back. That's your kidney. Here was a woman who would have happily turned that $14 million over to you in exchange for that little lump of flesh under your hand.

While you're at it, why don't you slide your other hand around behind you on the other side, because you've got two of them. In Erma's mind, you have $28 million worth of kidneys back there.

What are your eyes worth? What are your arms, your legs, your kidneys worth? A friend recently had a liver transplant, and the procedure cost over $180,000. What is your liver worth?

We tend to place a high value on those things that cost us a lot of money. But the reality is, the most important things in your life are things you got for free. Your ability to get out of bed in the morning and stand up on your feet, to breathe in the air and look out the window. Your ability to reason, to express yourself, to love, to be concerned for other people—these are things we have that are literally priceless. And yes, even our problems. My poverty was a buried treasure, just as our talents and gifts are buried treasures. As I said before:

Easter eggs—only these are Easter eggs that are spun from pure gold.

Whenever I catch myself having a pity party, I stop and think about all the things I have to be grateful for in my life, and realize how blessed I am. It's so easy to take for granted the things that matter most.

If you think you're having a bad day, try missing a few. Any day above ground is a good day.

Becoming Band Queen

I can't close this chapter without telling you how the Band Queen contest worked out.

When the evening finally came, I put on that gorgeous dress that Judy Boyd had loaned me, that I had unknowingly saved from our house fire by parking at a neighbor's house to avoid getting all saw-dusty. I don't mind telling you: in that borrowed gown, I felt like a million dollars.

The band played and played, and all of us Band Queen candidates began our beauty-pageant walk around the periphery of the gymnasium. Eventually the ballots were all collected and brought backstage, where a small team of people began counting them.

Soon we got word: it was a tie. They had counted the exact same number of votes for me and for a girl named Gail Harmon, who was a year ahead of me.

The teachers huddled to try and figure out what to do. This had never happened before. They couldn't declare it a tie between the two of us, because they only had one crown and one dozen roses. Someone was going to have to win. But which one?

Meanwhile my friend Carol Waugh, who was one of the girls counting votes in back, came over to me with some shocking news. "Rita," she whispered, "there's some voter fraud going on there!" While counting the ballots, they had noticed that there were more than a dozen votes for Gail that had been written in the exact same handwriting. Someone had stuffed the ballot box! They even knew who it was: a boy named Cecil, who was known to be sweet on Gail.

Gail had nothing to do with the bogus ballots; she didn't know anything about it. None of this was in any way her fault. All she knew was that the teachers had our fate in their hands—and that she might not win. Gail was a really sweet girl, and everybody loved her, including me. I didn't want her to be upset. At the same time, I so wanted to win myself.

To this day, I have no idea exactly why the decision went the way it did. I don't know if it was because Gail was a year older, or if the teachers had simply drawn one of our names from a hat, but whatever the reasons, in the end they gave the title to Gail.

I felt betrayed and cheated. Life had let me down.

Anytime you suffer an adversity, look for the gift. You may not see it right away, and in some cases, not even for quite a while. But with every adversity there is an equal or greater gift that will manifest itself sooner or later.

There was no way I could have possibly understood the meaning of that bitter disappointment, not at the time. It wasn't long, though, before I was able to see it in a whole different light. (As Paul Harvey was famous for saying, "And now, the rest of the story.")

Gail had a boyfriend who was a very nice guy, and soon after graduating from high school, they were married. She became pregnant right away. Less than a year later, when she was still just nineteen years old, Gail died of an aneurism while giving birth.

In her short life, there were so few things Gail Harmon could celebrate and cherish. This was her crowning moment—literally!—and I will always be so grateful that it happened for her.

Chapter 4

BUILDING BELIEF

In my senior year of high school, my home economics teacher, Mrs. Karleen Dean, who also served as my guidance counselor, sat me down and told me the facts of life about my future.

"Forget about college, Rita," she said, "you're just not college material. My advice to you is to concentrate on finding a good husband."

I know that when I tell this story, that sounds awful. How could she say such a mean thing? But she wasn't being mean; the truth is, she was right. I wasn't. I hadn't taken the preparatory classes—advanced math, trig, chemistry, things like that. What's more, in our generation not all that many high school graduates went on to college, especially not among the women. Nobody in my family ever had, that's for sure. I didn't really feel I had the academic aptitude to make college a likely track. And Lord knew I didn't have the financial resources to pay for it. Mrs. Dean was only saying what made sense. There was no reason to believe that I could pursue a successful college career.

And that right there, that word, was the real issue: *belief*.

When Mrs. Dean said I wasn't college material, I believed her, and as a result, I deferred to her judgment. When my classmates started looking at what colleges they might apply to, I didn't pursue the thought at all. I just let it go. And if that had been that, you wouldn't be reading this book, because there would have been no book to write.

Mind Your Mind

Most people think they think, but they don't actually think: they let other people think for them. If you don't choose what you think about, somebody else will choose it for you. Your thoughts are like your time: if you don't manage your time, someone else will manage it for you, and you'll live your life at the whim of others.

The capacity to truly think—to choose our own thoughts and think for ourselves—is an incredible gift that we've all been given by our Creator, and most of us never even unwrap the box, let alone take out what's inside and use it. Sue Grafton wrote this: "Thinking is hard work, which is why you don't see many people doing it." Albert Schweitzer was asked once, "Why do people think you're so smart?" and he said, "Well, I don't know. I just try to think once a day." Once a day—and that put him way ahead of the rest of the world.

Buckminster Fuller, the man behind the geodesic dome and the ahead-of-his-time design slogan "do more with less," and one of the most brilliant men of the twentieth century, experienced a great tragedy early in his life: his first child, a baby daughter, died from an illness. At the same time, he and his young wife were going through terrible financial struggles. Feeling like a complete failure, Fuller stood on the shore of Lake Michigan in the winter and was just about to throw himself in—figuring that at least his wife could live off the insurance money—when he suddenly stopped and made a radical decision: he decided to think.

Reasoning that he'd made a mess of his life by trying to following other people's thoughts, he decided it was time to figure out what *he* thought. For the next two years, he didn't speak a word: he wanted to make sure that when he opened his mouth, it would be his own thoughts that came out. And they were thoughts that changed the world.

I believe conforming to others' thoughts and ideas is one of the biggest strategic errors we can make. Conformity is the abdication of genuine belief: it is fitting yourself into the mold of beliefs formed by others. Conforming to other people's expectations is a serious strategic error. You've got the answers buried in you right now.

A Change in Plans

My acquiescence to Mrs. Dean's assessment of my poor academic prospects did not last long. A few months after my high school graduation, I made the decision to put Mrs. Dean's advice aside. I decided I was going to college.

A big part of the reason I decided to put myself on a track to a college career had to do with another person whom I believed in. Specifically, a boy.

When I was fourteen, there was a boy in my freshman English class named David Davenport. I liked him right away. I like to joke that I had several guys waiting in the wings in case this one didn't work out, but it's not really true. David and I dated off and on starting in our junior year. We went to our high school graduation together and after that started dating more seriously.

After graduating from high school I went looking for gainful employment. I was still working part-time at Woolworth's, Friday nights and Saturdays, and before long I found myself a regular weekday job, as I'll describe in a moment. At the same time, I was dating a college student, going to college ball games, and having regular glimpses of a kind of life that was very different from how I saw my own life would be like if I did not pursue a higher education.

David was a very motivating force for me. A serious and singularly determined student, he went through engineering school at Vanderbilt in only four years, which was unusual, and graduated with honors. When he started, we would see each other one or two nights a week. By his senior year we were lucky if it was once a week, because he was studying all the time. He was working really hard at getting that engineering degree, and I was in awe of him.

The fact that I was not in college gnawed at me. David and I were not engaged, but I knew he was the one I wanted to spend the rest of my life with. He was the kindest, smartest, best-looking, sweetest, most intelligent person I had ever been around, and the person I felt I could trust and respect. I loved him, always have, always will, and fully expected that I would marry him—and that posed a problem. You see, I figured that if I married a college graduate from Vanderbilt and did not have an advanced degree myself, it would not be long before he would outgrow me.

Instead, I wanted David to be married to someone he would be proud of, someone he had to run to keep up with. Someone who, someday, he would look at, poke the guy next to him with his elbow and say, "Hey, that's my lady up there on the stage."

I also wanted to be a significant person, because I was so proud of him. I believed in David, and that inspired me to believe in myself.

David encouraged and pushed me to make something out of myself. His mother was a single mom; she had lost her husband, gone to work, and always worked from then on. Because his mother worked, David naturally expected that I would too. He would say to me, "What do you plan to do with your life?" No one had ever asked me that before!

It didn't take long. I pretty quickly decided that I had to go to college, too. I wasn't sure exactly what I would do with my life (to answer David's question), but most of the time, at that point, I thought I would probably become a schoolteacher, because so many teachers had inspired me over the years.

Sometimes my dreams were more grandiose. I remember telling David, "If you don't marry me, you'll be sorry. Someday I'm going to be a fashion designer, or open my own boutique…" (I always had a passion for fashion) "…and I'm going to be *very* successful." I'm sure he got a good chuckle out of that. Of course, I never did become a fashion designer or open any boutiques. Sometimes, when we're aiming for our biggest life dreams, the best we can do is approximate. And most times, that's good enough. Time and circumstance will fill in the details, as long as we provide the general aim, the passion, the elbow grease, and the sweat equity.

Finding Work

It was all very well for me to decide I was going to college—but of course I couldn't afford it. I was going to have to earn some serious money for tuition, books, and whatever I would need to live on. I needed to go to work.

Many of the women who graduated from my high school went to work at Life & Casualty or the National Life Insurance Company. To get a job at either place, you had to be able to type at least forty words per minute. Try as I might, though, I could not get my typing speed up past about thirty words.

My mother's goal for me was to be a secretary and work in an office. In her view, secretaries wore hose and high heels, dressed nicely, and went to work in nice offices. "Momma," I said, "that's just not what I want to do. I'd rather *be* a boss than *have* one." But she was so disappointed. It seemed to her that all the girls in the neighborhood had gotten secretarial jobs. I did not make the grade. As I look back, I can see a very good reason I couldn't type: evidently God knew that if I could, that's what I would have ended up doing my whole life. While being a secretary is a noble profession, I would have *been* a secretary instead of *needing* one. At the time, though, it was a major disappointment.

This was not the last time I would try out for a job, and fail. The next time it happened, it took me years to recover from the blow to my own self-esteem. Sometimes it felt like building my belief in myself was a one-step-forward, two-steps-backward proposition. But I wasn't about to quit.

Instead, I got a job at the National Life Insurance Company sorting and delivering the mail. Soon I'd gotten to know everybody in the building. Meanwhile, every lunch hour I went and practiced on that typewriter. But I seem to have the digital dexterity of an amoeba, and my fingers often got stuck in home row. I never did make it to forty words a minute.

After working in the mail room for a while, I got to be a junior underwriter, which was not as important as being a secretary or typist (and didn't earn as much, either), but still, it was a step up from the mail room. I worked there for two years, saving every penny I could toward the college expenses I expected to have, whenever that would be.

Meanwhile, I started taking classes at night school in order to get a jump on some of my credits. I would take the bus to work in the morning, walk from there to night school, and Daddy would pick me up at school and drive me home, cussing out the other drivers all the way. Among the required courses for my degree were Interior Design, Economics, English, Math … and Psychology.

Psychology was fascinating. It was here that I was first introduced to William James and began to develop an appreciation for the power of our thoughts. This was a concept that became very important to me in time, and in the years to come I would meet many people who would greatly contribute to this direction of thinking for me, especially my friend Calvin Lehew.

Birds of a Feather

David had gone to church and Sunday school with a boy named Wayne King, who had since gotten married to a girl named Daisy, who later went on to create a wonderful little restaurant in Nashville called Miss Daisy's Tearoom. Daisy had a backer: her tearoom was owned by a man named Calvin Lehew, who became a good friend and important figure in my life.

Calvin was an entrepreneur's entrepreneur. When I was a kid, I had always bragged about my big dreams and how I was going to be rich and successful. But Calvin was the first person I knew who had genuinely started from humble beginnings and actually made something remarkable of himself. Both his parents died when Calvin was still a teenager; Calvin's father had been friends with Sen. Albert Gore Sr. and his wife Pauline, who later recommended that Calvin become a senatorial page. Calvin even baby-sat for future Vice President Al Gore Jr. (he liked to joke that he was Vice President Gore's first bodyguard) and in time got to know five U.S. presidents. Calvin later bought an old mattress factory in Franklin, right outside Nashville, and converted it into a row of boutiques that he called The Factory. The Factory also had performance halls and courted a lot of the country music acts that were gaining popularity in Nashville. It was a huge success.

Calvin talked a lot about the "science of mind"—writers like James Allen (*As a Man Thinketh*), Wallace Wattles (*The Science of Getting Rich*), Napoleon Hill (*Think and Grow Rich*), Dale Carnegie (*How to Win Friends and Influence People*), Norman Vincent Peale (*The Power of Positive Thinking*), and Earl Nightingale (*The Strangest Secret*). I had already encountered some of these writers in my psychology studies, but now they took on a whole new meaning, and they helped build my belief in myself and gave me the drive to push forward. "When you set a goal or intention," Calvin told me, "automatically little miracles start taking place. Your hunches and intuition, also called illuminations, will tell you what to do. You'll start receiving phone calls and seeing people." Through Calvin's example I began to realize that these abstract ideas I'd read about were pragmatic, living truths. Getting to know Calvin Lehew was a pivotal experience, and we have remained friends for life. He and his wife, Marilyn, are godparents to our two kids.

Miss Daisy's Tearoom was one of the shops in Carter's Court, a development of Calvin's that preceded The Factory, and whenever David and I went to Nashville (which was as often as we could) we would go to Franklin and eat at Miss Daisy's, because the food there was fabulous. We became friends with Daisy, and at one point I encouraged Daisy and Calvin to write a cookbook. The idea had never occurred to them, but they did it. It was called *Recipes from Miss Daisy's*, and it became a runaway best-seller and a classic that people still refer to decades later. (In fact, I later learned it was Erma Bombeck's favorite cookbook.) More cookbooks followed, including *Miss Daisy Entertains, Miss Daisy's Blue Ribbon Desserts, Miss Daisy Celebrates Tennessee, Miss Daisy's Healthy Southern Cooking*, and more. All in all, they have sold more than one and a half million copies.

Later in life I would draw on this experience to create cookbooks of my own. Meanwhile, I drew inspiration from her example. Daisy had so much charisma and Southern charm; she had been brought up in a well-to-do family, knew how to dress and exuded confidence. And she was always so friendly and sweet to all her customers. I studied her behavior, analyzing her personality and the role it played in the success of their tearoom (in addition, of course, to how good the food was). At times I found myself emulating her. She served as a role model in a few crucial moments, when I used her outgoing personality as an example to overcome my own shyness and insecurity. Acting as if I, too, had been raised within a prominent circle of family and friends, I would tell myself to "work the room" as she worked her tearoom by being gracious, complimentary, and engaging.

There's a saying in the South: *You lay down with dogs, you're gonna get fleas.* We are so much a product of who we spend time with. According to Judith Harris, author of the enormously influential book *The Nurture Assumption*, as much as 80 percent of what happens to your kids will be determined by who they hang around with. Powerful peers and role models are such an important part of building your own belief in yourself and your possibilities. Later on, in my broadcasting career, I had ample opportunity to spend time with all sorts of successful people, and they certainly inspired and helped shape who I've become and what I've accomplished.

If you haven't yet met the kinds of successful entrepreneurs, celebrities, and other people who can raise your expectations and teach you success skills, you can create much the same impact by reading the biographies of famous people who have achieved the kinds of things in life that you want to achieve. We can't always find powerful successful people to hang around in the flesh, but the role models you need to inspire you and build your own belief are never more than a page away. Calvin recently wrote a book, coauthored with Stowe Shockey, titled *Flying High*, which teaches about health, happiness, wealth, and a deep joy of living. Calvin has been a lifelong mentor of mine, and reading his book can give you the same opportunity.

Taking on College

The time finally came to take my SATs. Because I had taken some extension courses, I was now regarded as a transfer student, and therefore, according to Tennessee rules, I had to hit a minimum score on my SATs that was somewhat higher than I would have had to hit if I were coming in simply as a brand-new student.

Once again, as with my typing tests at the insurance company, I did not test well and didn't make it. This was yet another blow to my still-fragile belief in myself. As it turned out, I scored exactly one point below the minimum I needed—and I didn't get into college after all, at least not then. When Mrs. Dean had told me I wasn't college material, in my mind she had been dead right. Here I was, flunking my SATs!

I could have quit right then and there, and I almost did. But I had more reasons to go to school than not to go to school. I decided to push on. This was a state school, after all, and while they could delay my entrance, they couldn't totally deny it. Plus, I had made all A's in my evening classes. So the following semester, a full two years after graduating from high school, I was finally accepted into a degree program at Middle Tennessee State University, where I would spend the next three years pursuing a bachelor's degree in education with a minor in science.

Those three years were grueling. I went straight through everything I needed to get my degree, and to make it all work I knew I would sometimes have to hold down at least two and maybe three part-time jobs, which is exactly what I ended up doing. Fortunately, the head of the Home Economics department, Miss Putnam, seemed to believe in me (which was a serious boost to my self-esteem), and she asked me to be her student assistant. That was one job. I also worked in the school cafeteria: job #2. Meanwhile, I was still working part-time at the Woolworth's counter (job #3), and I found more besides. I decorated cakes. I did flower arranging. I did decorating. I did all kinds of things to earn the money I needed to make my way through school.

At one point I worked at a department store on the fashion board, and while I was there I also got a part-time job working as a mannequin, modeling clothes in the window, and sometimes right out on the floor. I would stand there in an outfit without moving for what seemed like hours, and people would walk by without realizing I was a live human. I overheard all kinds of interesting conversations. I got pretty good at this. I knew how to concentrate, and I would just zone out. As I told a magazine writer years later who asked me about this, "Clearly, I was destined to be a dummy."

One time I was standing out on the showroom floor, dressed in a ski outfit, and two women came up and started looking over my clothes. One of them peered at my face and said to her friend, "I just cannot believe how lifelike these mannequins are. Why, you can see freckles there! And look, they've painted on faint little veins on the backs of her hands!"

I stood there thinking, "You have *got* to be kidding."

Suddenly the woman said, "I have *got* to try on this jacket," and she started unzipping my ski jacket! It was hot in that store and all I had on underneath the jacket was a bra. What could I do? I moved—and the woman fainted dead away.

What a commotion. The manager came over and when he found out what had happened, he told me, "I don't care if they strip you naked, in the future, don't move." I'm pretty sure he was kidding.

Along with all the jobs I also managed to get a small

scholarship. In fact, it was the very same Mrs. Dean who'd told me I wasn't college material who steered me toward this scholarship and helped me apply for it. (Ironically, even though Mrs. Dean had discouraged me from ever going to college, she believed in me—and she played a big part in my success.) That scholarship wasn't much, just a few hundred dollars, but it made a huge difference and I would never forget it.

In the summer of my last year of school, I took a speech class. All the other students were big strong male athletes, making up needed credits by cramming in some summer classes so they wouldn't be academically burdened during the sports season. Our teacher was tough and wouldn't allow his students to use note cards, not even for our twenty-minute final-exam speech. (How many times since then have I heard people say they were astounded that I don't use notes when I give a speech—another example of an adversity becoming a gift!)

I didn't think I had any particular talent in this area, and being the only female in the class, I felt a bit intimidated. I suppose I must have been trying to compensate: for the class's speech contest I prepared a speech titled "The Natural Superiority of Women Over Men." (This was before the days of Betty Friedan, Gloria Steinem, and Women's Liberation.) I gathered up all sorts of statistics about newborn girls, their abilities and relative mortality rates, how they were stronger and had a better chance of survival, had more acute skills earlier on, and so forth. It must have been compelling. To my great surprise, I won the contest.

My jock classmates were blown away. One of them later told me, "I didn't sleep all night, thinking about what you said, because it was so accurate."

I went on to enter a regional speech contest, but when my turn came I got so nervous that I spoke too fast, and I finished fifteen seconds short of the allotted time, which disqualified me. My professor told me I could have stood there and cleared my throat for those last fifteen seconds and still won, but I was too rattled to realize it at the time.

This experience gave me a strong clue that speaking was something I might want to take a look at pursuing. Apparently I had a gift of some sort in this area. But it never occurred to me that one could actually earn a living doing this. That would come later.

The Power of Belief

In my television interviews I would always ask people, "What do you think made you successful?" One of the most memorable times I asked that question was when I interviewed Muhammad Ali, and he told me about creating his famous affirmation, "I am the greatest," and how he used it to change his life.

In the beginning of his career, Ali was not all that great a boxer. He certainly wasn't *the greatest*. But he kept repeating that positive assertion, that "I am" statement, as if the goal had already been achieved: *I am the greatest*. And in time he did indeed become the greatest boxer the world had ever seen.

Your mind only knows what you tell it. You can tell your mind that you're not going to be successful, and you certainly won't be. Or you can tell your mind, "I am going to be successful *no matter what*." That *no matter what* attitude is so key. When Ali used to say that, he wasn't boasting or bragging. He was exercising that *no matter what* attitude.

A woman named Phyllis came on my television show once and did a cooking segment. Phyllis had a unique brand of self-deprecating humor and she was very entertaining. She described herself as "ugly, divorced, with five children, almost no education, and living on welfare." However I knew there was more to the story, because she had actually become quite successful. I knew that at one time in her past, she had cleaned office buildings to get by, and I asked her about that, and about how she had pulled herself out of that life and become so successful.

At night, she said, she would go around this one office building cleaning all the rooms. One night, she happened to see a book in one of the trashcans she was cleaning. The book was called *The Magic of Believing*, by Claude Bristol. She took it home and devoured it.

"After I read that book," she said, "you know what? I was still ugly. I was still on welfare. I still had five kids. I was still divorced. But the book taught me one thing: *quit comparing yourself to the beautiful people of Hollywood, because they don't exist.*"

Bristol's book told Phyllis, "Protect your thoughts and turn them into achievements.... Apply the power of your imagination to overcome obstacles." It also urged the reader to find something she was good at, and become great at it.

"The only thing I could think of that I was good at," reported Phyllis," was being funny. I'd always been told I was funny. I was voted wittiest in my high school. I thought, maybe I could go down to the local pub, after I finished cleaning up, and see if I could get on the microphone and tell a few stories and jokes. Hey, I'd do it for free." And that's exactly what she did. She started going down to that pub regularly after work and practicing her skill at telling jokes … and in time, Phyllis Diller earned millions for telling jokes.

I spoke at the same conference once with Buckminster Fuller and referred to him as "a genius." Later he amended this statement by telling the audience, "*Everybody's* a genius. There are just some of us who are less damaged than others." Most of us have been damaged by the negative beliefs of those around us, starting from when we were little, even from before we were born. It's up to us to reverse that negative programming—and it starts with believing in yourself.

You are worthy of success and will enjoy success to the extent—and *only* to the extent—that you believe in yourself. If you don't, everyone can spot it. Contrary to popular belief, people are not fools. If you don't believe in yourself, it shows on your face and everyone else can see it. And if you don't believe in you, why should they? They're having enough trouble as it is maintaining their own belief in themselves! Commit to seeing *yourself* in your highest possibilities, and act *as if*!

The power of belief is phenomenal. It's the most important component of success. The Bible says "As a man thinketh, so is he." Now, I've got to come clean with something here: though I've gone to church and Sunday school all my life, I am *not* an especially good student of the Bible. I can't quote you chapter and verse, like a Joel Osteen or a Joyce Meyer. But that's one passage I *do* know (it's Proverbs 23:7), and I know that there are an awful lot of examples throughout the Bible of that truth.

There is another powerful expression of that idea, attributed to the Pulitzer Prize–winning historian James Truslow Adams:

The greatest discovery of my generation is that man can alter his life simply by altering his attitudes of mind.

You *can* change your life simply by changing your attitude. In fact, you can alter it *dramatically*.

A Footnote to College
One day in 1984, eighteen years after graduating from Middle Tennessee State University, I got a letter from my alma mater saying they were going to present me with their Distinguished Alumnus Award. What's more, they said, I was the youngest person they had ever selected for this honor. They were going to hold a banquet with eight hundred people in attendance, and they wanted to know if I would help them put together a slide presentation of my life. Also, would I be able to attend the dinner and say a few words?

Would I ever! I certainly did attend that dinner—and I invited Mrs. Dean to be there with me. They had made a brass plaque with my image on it, which they hung in the student union building, listing some of my accomplishments underneath it. While I was there, reflecting on how much my education meant to me, I was grateful to be able to establish a special scholarship to help needy students. It felt great to pay it forward. That scholarship is still there today:

the Rita Davenport Human Sciences Scholarship at Middle Tennessee State University, College of Behavioral and Health Sciences, Department of Human Sciences. To be eligible, applying students:

> *Must be majoring in one of the human sciences areas,*
> *must have at least 30 semester hours earned, and*
> *must have minimum 2.8 GPA with financial need*
> *and demonstrated leadership in the areas of Human*
> *Sciences, campus life, and community involvement.*
> *They must establish meaningful professional goals.*
> *They need to be a full-time student during semesters for*
> *which scholarship is funded.*

And while this isn't an official part of the requirements, I would add this: *They must believe in themselves.*

Twelve years later, in 1996, I was honored and humbled to be invited to Middle Tennessee State University once again, this time to give the university's commencement address for that year, where I would be addressing an audience of some 16,000 people. I invited Mrs. Dean to join me in that event as well, and she did. We remain good friends to this day.

Chapter 5

THE POWER OF LOVE
... AND SELF-RESPECT

David Davenport and I were married in the summer of 1966, just as I graduated from college. (As I say when talking to people in sales, I married my high school sweetheart, but only after we'd both been through college: it took me six years to close him.) Immediately after my commencement exercises we moved to Daytona Beach, Florida, where David had an engineering job with General Electric as part of NASA and the bold effort to put a man on the moon—that "impossible dream" that President Kennedy had initiated with his daring declaration to Congress in 1961. It was an exciting thing to be a part of, and I was so proud of David for it. All in all, it was an exciting adventure that we were on. I had left home and started my new life.

And I was miserable.

I missed my family. I didn't know anyone in Florida but David, and I was homesick. We thought David was going to be transferred to Houston later that fall, so it didn't seem there was any point in applying for a teaching position. I had no friends, no job, and nothing to do.

So instead, I applied for a job at Florida Power & Light Company as a *consumer service specialist*. This was an interesting job and when I learned about it, I did that thing I'd so often been told not to do: I got my hopes up. As a consumer services specialist, I would be going to schools, businesses, and other organizations, demonstrating methods of energy conservation and the use and care of appliances. I would talk about indoor and outdoor lighting techniques, interior design work, and all sorts of things. If a company was opening up a new business at the mall, say, selling gas barbecues, I might go in and demonstrate how to use the barbecues. The job was mostly all about giving demonstrations and presentations, which sounded like fun. I was certainly qualified for the position, and I was sure I'd be good at it, so I was quite excited when I applied for it. And then they rejected my application.

I couldn't believe it. I didn't get the job!

Being turned down by Florida Power & Light Company was a serious blow to my already fragile state of self-respect. I had been *sure* I would qualify for this position, but apparently I was wrong. Apparently, I just wasn't up to par. In reality, the only reason they turned me down was that the job required traveling one day per month to another city, including an overnight stay, and because I was married my would-be employers had decided (without bothering to ask me first) that this wouldn't be a possibility for me, because traveling could put a strain on anyone's marriage. (Remember, this was a long time ago!) But they didn't tell me this. In fact, I didn't even learn about this until several years later, when a friend (who *had* gotten the job when I didn't) finally fessed up and told me. Meanwhile, I was devastated.

This was the first time I hadn't worked since I was twelve years old, when I first started cleaning houses and baby-sitting for extra money. Now, that had been quite the first-time-employment experience. The woman paid me five dollars a week, and that was really good money back then. And boy, did I earn it. In addition to cleaning, I was also cooking her dinner. On top of that, one of her kids was a bed wetter, so every day after school I would change and launder the sheets, clean up the house, wash the dishes from the night before, and then get dinner on the table. It wasn't much, fish sticks or hot dogs and beans, but it was a pretty full slate for a twelve-year-old, so I decided to ask for a raise. When she declined to give it to me, I quit. At the age of twelve, I had enough self-respect to know that I was worth more than a dollar a day. Even then my instincts told me that people will treat you the way you *let* them treat you.

And now here I was, at twenty-three—and I couldn't get hired. I was mortified.

David was commuting an hour each way to Cape Canaveral. Basically, after the apartment was clean and I had dinner planned, I would sit around the house all day, reading and feeling sorry for myself. During our first six weeks in Daytona Beach, I read twenty-six classic books I'd always wanted to read but had never had the time.

Then one day I got a kick in the pants. I heard the mailman dropping our mail in the box and popped out to get it. I thought I was doing a good job of putting on a happy face, but it must have not been all that good, or else he was an especially acute observer, because he glanced at me and said, "Little lady, you don't look happy."

Busted.

"I'm *not* happy," I said. "I don't know anyone here. I have nothing to do. I'm homesick. My husband and I dated for six years and he's the love of my life—but he's busy at work every day putting a man on the moon, and I'm stuck here at home, miserable."

I really hadn't planned to pour out my entire life story to the mailman, but that all spilled out before I could stop myself.

He just looked at me with a pointed expression and said, "Little lady, you're going to be as happy as you make up your mind to be."

Whoa. He had a good point there. Later I learned that he

had gotten this piece of wisdom from Abraham Lincoln—a man who certainly knew a thing or two about happiness and unhappiness. But at the moment, all I knew was that my mailman was a genius.

After he went off to deliver his mail (and possibly his wisdom) to the next apartment building on the block, I sat down and thought about what he said. Was my problem that I hadn't made up my own mind to be happy? It didn't take me long (like a few seconds) to realize that this was exactly the case. I had thought my husband could make me happy. I don't know exactly how I was thinking that would happen … maybe that he'd come home from work every day and sprinkle happiness dust over me? Right. Earth to Rita. Hello?

I realized that it was me, and only me, who was responsible for finding those things that would fulfill me, engage me, excite me, and make me happy—responsible for finding those things and then *doing* those things. My own happiness was up to me. David couldn't "make" me happy. No other person on earth could do that.

The Key to a Happy Marriage

To me marriage is about two things. One is having children and raising a family. That is an incredible thing, and we'll talk about it more in another chapter. The other purpose of marriage is the one I want to talk about here: I believe that what marriage is really about is two people spending their lives helping each other become the great that we are all capable of being.

But help each other though we might, ultimately we are each our own person. Nobody can make you happy. You have to get in touch with your own greatness. I believe one of the greatest missions each of us has in this life is to love other people. But you cannot truly love another unless you first learn to accept and love yourself. And this may be the single most important factor in the building of a successful marriage.

Getting married is easy. *Staying* married is the challenge. People have often asked me what is the secret of the vibrancy and longevity of my marriage to David. Here is how I generally answer that question: "It's easy. I remind my husband on occasion that I'm kind, I'm sweet, I'm loving, and I'm a good cook. That, and I've also been known to make a lot of money. Besides, what could he find in another woman that I can't have fixed?" As Dolly Parton says, "If it's baggin', saggin', or draggin', you can nip it, tuck it, or suck it!"

I joke.

I asked David one Valentine's Day not long ago, "After all these years of marriage, what is it about me that still turns you on?" He thought about it for a while. Okay, I'll be honest with you: it was a *long* while. Finally he said, "Well, Honey, you are so clean—you're always taking a bubble bath and putting on all those fancy lotions." Hmph. So I went out the next day and I bought myself a black lace $150 Vanity Fair peignoir-and-negligee set. That night I walked out of the bathroom and into the bedroom, stood in front of him, stretched out my arms and twirled around like a ballerina. You know what he said? "Well, any friend of Zorro's is a friend of mine."

Okay, he jokes too. You have to keep a sense of humor about these things. But all joking aside, I think that one of the core secrets to a long and successful marriage is simply this:

Both partners need to have their own distinct identity—and to keep holding onto, growing, and developing that identity.

Each of us is here with a unique assignment. We each have a purpose, as I said before, and we are given the requisite talents and gifts we need to fulfill that purpose. Those who don't use the gifts they were sent here to use live their lives with a constant undercurrent of frustration, because there's a little homing device inside them that's constantly whispering, "I know you're over *here*—but you're supposed to be over *there*." Whether or not they know exactly what that feeling is or why they're having it, they cannot escape it, and as a result, they never feel good about themselves.

And marriage to another person, no matter how wonderful, loving, and devoted that person may be, cannot bridge that gap or fill that void.

I think this is a common problem in Hollywood, as well as in the performing industry, in politics, sports, in the world of direct selling, and in any marriage where one of the two people is regularly in the limelight. In a situation like that, the second person, the one who is not in the limelight, has to be the stronger one. And David has always been that for me.

I don't think David has ever felt threatened by any of the accolades and public visibility that have been an inevitable part of the various careers I've pursued. Many times we've been in restaurants and had people come up to us wanting to chat or have their picture taken with me. (I don't say that to brag; it's not about me, it just comes with the territory of being a broadcaster or a company president.) I've been on stage hundreds of times, on television, and in the public eye in one way or another for decades. And there's never been a time that David seemed to feel my success took anything away from *his* success. Why not? Because he has always had a sense of who he is, an internal gyroscope of confidence that doesn't depend on anything external, from me or anyone else. (In fact, he always seems to find it amusing. He knows very well that I don't take being in the limelight too seriously, and neither does he.)

I believe we all develop that sense of our self, of our purpose and identity, much earlier in life than people often realize. Many times, though, we allow marriage to lower our expectations for ourselves, because we think someone else is going to fulfill our needs and make us happy. And many women, especially, fail to reach their potential or have genuine fulfillment in their lives because they're afraid that if they became "too successful," they might threaten their husband or significant other and end up in constant conflict—or alone. I have seen women who had immense talent, who could have made far more money or gained greater recognition and accomplishment than their husbands, step back from doing what they could out of the fear that if they did, the husband would resent it. And while I hate to say it, they may have been right about that—which is a terrible thing. A woman should be made to feel that it's okay if she makes more money or earns greater recognition than her husband. (It also doesn't hurt to make him aware that a major incentive to becoming successful is to honor and complement *him*.)

A man of quality is not threatened by a woman of equality. Besides, there is plenty enough money and recognition to go around.

And men, let me tell you a secret: there is nothing sexier than a rich woman.

David has given me two things: wings and roots. If he had not been so supportive for all these years, I would never have been able to do all the things I've done, and I am so grateful to have him in my life.

Social Work

We ended up staying in Daytona Beach for three years, and not long after that conversation with the mailman, I did in fact get a job, thanks to my friend and neighbor Mary Ellen DeLoache, who was a social worker. I started working as a social worker with the Aid to Dependent Children (ADC) program. When I told my oldest and dearest friend, Regina Merryman, who grew up across the street from me, that I'd gotten a job as a social worker, she said, "Rita, you've been a social worker all your life!" I didn't think it'd been so apparent.

My job consisted, mostly, of going on calls to young mothers who were in the program to observe the particulars about how they were living and offer them support. I spent most days driving around in our '61 Chevrolet and dropping in on these "clients." That old Chevy had no air conditioning, and this was Florida, with its heat and high humidity. Often I'd be drenched in sweat by noon and have to go home to change clothes.

Sometimes I was very tough on those young mothers, because they couldn't pull anything over on me. Often they would have an attitude that said, "Poor me, I'm in such a tough situation, and I can't do anything about it." I wouldn't buy into it. Yes, they were often dirt poor, but that didn't cut much ice with me. Heck, I had been raised poor. I grew up bathing in a #2 washtub, and I knew that just because you're poor doesn't mean you can't keep your children clean. It doesn't take a fortune to buy a bar of soap. Sometimes I would bring soap with me on a home visit and leave it behind, just so I knew—and they knew that that I knew—they had no excuse to not take a bath and see that their kids were clean, too.

I almost got myself assaulted one time because I refused to buy into hard-luck stories. I had driven one day out into the middle of a huge orange grove to a makeshift bar they had set up to confront a man who'd gotten one of my "clients" pregnant. Evidently this guy had just gotten out of prison, after serving time for who knows how long for who knows what crime, and he was out here drinking with his buddies while this poor woman was sitting at home trying to figure out how to manage her life.

I found the ramshackle dive where the men were all getting potted, parked my old Chevy just outside the place, hopped out, and headed into the bar. When I entered the place, it was something like one of those scenes in a Western, where the white-hatted sheriff walks into the bar and all conversation immediately stops, along with the obligatory piano. Here I was, small frame, naïve, long blonde hair, twenty-three years old, surrounded by a small herd of big, tough burly guys.

"Hey, you there!" I called out when I saw the feller I was gunning for.

He turned slowly around and looked at me.

"I just came from (the girl's name's) house, and want to know, just what exactly are your intentions?"

He stared at me. I think he may have been wondering

if I was real, or if he was a lot drunker even than he thought. Or maybe he wasn't thinking anything at all.

"Now you listen up," I yelled at him, "because I'm telling you right here and now, you're gonna do the right thing and marry this poor girl!"

The rest of the guys in the bar started hooting and hollering, whether at me or at the guy I wasn't sure. A few of them practically fell off their stools, they were laughing so hard.

Later on I asked myself how I could be so stupid to walk in there by myself and start dressing down a big drunk ex-con with nobody else around but his buddies. The truth was, I had high expectations for this man. I wanted him to be more responsible, and I believed and hoped he could be.

I'll never forget one home I visited, a few months after I'd started this job. It was the most pitiful situation I'd ever seen. The woman was essentially broke, unemployed, and had several children with another one on the way. Aside from being pregnant she was also fairly overweight. On top of that, she was mildly handicapped, mentally, and was completely on her own, since the children's father was at the moment doing time in Raiford state prison. Her home had no indoor plumbing and there were filthy clothes everywhere with urine and feces all over them. There were maggots in the dishes that filled the sink. The place was just horrible.

I told her, "Look, I'm gonna help you, but you have got to do your part, too."

I laid out for her what she was going to have to do to keep up her end of the deal.

"I know how you feel," I said, "because I've been there. I've been poor as dust. Here's what I found, though: you'll be happier, and your kids will be healthier, if this place is clean and they're getting enough food from your welfare check. I know you don't have much, but you've got to do the best you can with what you have. I promise you, I will get you this check—but you've got to use it for them."

I left, wondering how much of this had sunk in and if there would be any change at all the next time I came to see her. I talked about this woman to one of my coworkers, Judy Ellis, and told her I wanted to bring her with me when I returned. "Judy," I said, "you have got to see this house. It's the worst thing I've ever seen." The truth was, I couldn't face going there a second time by myself.

It was Christmas when I visited the woman again, this time with Judy in tow. I practically cringed as we walked through the front door, fearing the worst—and I almost couldn't believe what I saw.

The woman had scrubbed the floors to the point where she had taken off some of the paint. Everything was spit-shine clean. She had laid out newspapers like a tablecloth on her table, and the whole place was neatened up and as clean as could be. What's more, the children were clean, and so was she. And to top it all off, she had put up a scraggly little tree in the corner, decorating it with little rags and ribbons tied around the branches in an effort to create the feeling of ornaments.

Judy gaped at the place. Out of the corner of her mouth she quietly said, "Rita, this is nowhere near as bad as you said!"

"I know!" I whispered back. "But it sure was the last time I was here."

This poor woman had practically nothing going for her, but she had listened to everything I told her and taken it to heart. Nobody had ever given her that kind of direction before, and I could see the change it had made in her. There was a new light in her, and I knew exactly what it was: self-respect. Someone had raised the bar for her.

As leaders, as businesspeople, and simply as *people*, period, one of our jobs in life is to see other people in their highest possibility, to provide them a high-morale-producing environment, and raise the bar of their own sense of themselves.

I did this work for about a year and learned an enormous amount about the power of love and self-respect in the process. In the future, I would become quite involved in efforts to help victims of domestic violence, and a lot of the impulse to do that started there in the poor homes of central Florida.

High School

After a year of working with the ADC program I had to get out of social work, because I was giving everything away. (David claims he was down to three pair of underwear at this point.) I had come to realize that welfare wasn't the answer; giving handouts wasn't making any real, lasting difference in people's lives. It was more valuable to give the person a hand up than a handout, and to show people how to take care of themselves. What made a genuine difference was giving them higher expectations, and I wanted to do that by pursuing the teaching career I had originally planned.

I started working as a substitute teacher in the local public school system and soon a full-time position became available in vocational education, what was then called "Home Ec." I taught there for the next two years, in one of the first integrated schools in that area.

I loved, *loved* mentoring these students. They often came to our house and—especially since David and I did not yet have any children of our own—this was absolutely captivating for me. Many of my students were African American, and I think they got a kick out of this hillbilly white lady from Tennessee. I adored them, and they taught me much.

I had one little student, a foster child, who had never seen the ocean, although she lived only three miles from the beach. I found out that she was being treated terribly by her foster mother, treated like an indentured servant. I took her out in my old Chevrolet one day, during a school break, and treated her to her first experience of walking on a beach. One of the heartbreaks of that job was that I could not always follow my students long enough to learn how their stories came out in the end—but this was one case where I did. That little child did eventually get out from under the thumb of that terrible foster mother, and today she has a good job at a junior college in the Daytona Beach area. I loved hearing from her again recently and learning about all she has accomplished.

This was now 1967 leading into 1968, and that spring racial tensions in Florida got as hot as they did everywhere in the country, when Martin Luther King was assassinated in early April. I remember the day vividly. People were burning buildings all around us; some of the teachers' tires got slashed and even had their cars burned. I didn't have any problems, though; for whatever reason, people were careful to leave me alone. I think they knew that I loved them—their culture, their personalities, and just who they were.

Supposedly I was working as a high school teacher, but the truth was, I was doing the same thing I'd been doing as a social worker: caring for these kids, nurturing them, and most of all, teaching them how to love and respect themselves.

Walking on the Moon

In the summer of 1969 Neil Armstrong and Buzz Aldrin walked on the moon and I had my first walk on something that sure looked like the moon to me.

In the aftermath of the historic Apollo 11 mission to the lunar surface, David was transferred to Phoenix. This was no accident. He had realized that once they'd met that epic goal of putting a man on the moon and the great push was behind us, there would be engineers who would end up sweeping floors while they looked for jobs. He'd had the foresight to plan for this and had taken a job working with a computer division of General Electric in Phoenix.

I'd never set foot in Arizona before, and I hadn't expected to, not in my twenties, anyway. I thought Arizona was where people went to die. (Although I'm sure we must have ridden through it on that cross-country train ride when I was six years old, I had no memory of it.) The day David and I drove our car across the New Mexico–Arizona border on Route I-10 I thought, "Well this might not be the end of the world, but I'll bet you can see it from here!" My Lord, you could see clear out for a hundred miles. And if I stood on a tuna can, I bet I could see *two* hundred miles. It looked to me like five hundred thousand acres of kitty litter. You could watch your dog run away all day long.

As soon as we got settled, I enrolled in school again to get my master's degree at Arizona State University. I had actually started working on this while still in Florida, just the same way I had gotten a jump on my bachelor's degree in Tennessee, by taking some extension classes. Now it was time to pursue it in earnest.

A few weeks later, I got a job at Phoenix College as director of the child development division and the onsite nursery school / daycare center, where I would be working with two-, three-, and four-year-olds for the next year.

I loved, loved, *loved* working with these kids, especially since I didn't yet have any children of my own. (These were the ones who, to their parents' surprise and possibly chagrin, soon started "talking Southern.") Most of them were there all day long for extended day care. The supervisors who had been running the center before me didn't believe in giving these kids hugs when they arrived or left, or having any kind of physical contact or displays of affection. Right away I thought, *That's gonna have to change*, and I immediately introduced the idea that it was okay, when appropriate, to give the kids a hug.

I believe human beings have a need for physical touch that is just as vital as the need for nutrition. We need three hugs a day just to keep from becoming weird, every bit as much as we need niacin or vitamin B_{12}.

There was a fascinating and much-quoted study conducted at Ohio State University in 1980 that revealed something fascinating about the effect of physical affection and its impact on health.[9] (This was more than a decade *after* I started working at the center for childhood development at the college, so of course I didn't know about this yet; but I didn't need any scientific corroboration.) Researchers were feeding a number of rabbits a high-fat, high-cholesterol diet in order to study the progress of atherosclerosis. They naturally expected that all the rabbits would develop the disease, not only because that seemed a common-sense sort of cause and effect but also because previous studies had shown that this would reliably occur. But it didn't, at least, not entirely.

All of the rabbits did develop a thickening of their arterial walls, but not uniformly so. In fact, for absolutely no apparent reason, one particular subgroup developed 60 percent less atherosclerosis than the rest. They checked and rechecked all their figures, all the specs of the nutrition given and every conceivable variable, and could not figure out what could possibly account for the difference. That is, until one researcher finally noticed that when those particular rabbits were fed, they were taken from their cages, stroked, petted, and talked to by one of the scientists. This had to be a coincidence, they reasoned. The idea that simply petting a rabbit could cause a profound change in a predictable biochemical disease process seemed about as scientific as the idea that you could have good luck by ... well, by petting a rabbit's foot.

They got some new rabbits and repeated the experiments. All the new rabbits were treated identically—except that one small group were taken from their cages a few times a day to be petted, stroked, and talked to. Once again, those rabbits showed a 60 percent lower incidence of that vascular problem.

They did it a third time. And you'll never guess what happened. They got the same results.

A friend of mine worked for a while as a volunteer at an orphanage in postwar Japan with very young children who were orphans of war casualties, and she described something that had amazed her there. "We had babies dying, Rita," she said, "and we didn't know why. They all had symptoms of a severe deficiency, like kwashiorkor or marasmus. But here was the strange thing: they were all well fed, clean, and warm."

Eventually, she said, they realized what was happening:

they had so many children to take care of, that they didn't have enough personnel to hold those babies, to touch them and cuddle them. When they did, the babies improved.

When someone touches you, it increases hemoglobin production and lowers your blood pressure. Now, I'm not saying we should all slobber all over each other, but there is a need to be touched in this world. The reason nurses use a cotton swab with alcohol is not only to make it antiseptic but also because the patient needs to be touched. When a patient is anesthetized, someone's hand is on that person all the time. All good health care practitioners understand this instinctively, as do all good teachers, parents, and spouses.

Why do people stay in abusive relationships? It's terrible to say, but the truth is, sometimes we would rather be abused than not be touched at all. I believe the number one fear we have is to be alone. If you're lonely right now, do something about it. Take charge of your life. Be proactive. Go out and make some friends. Volunteer to help others. The benefits are huge! There's no good reason to be by yourself, no good reason to be lonely in a world where so many people are crying out to be touched and loved. We've become so highly technologically developed in our society that we sometimes forget that we need the physical, tangible experience of love from other people. Every person on the earth is crying out, albeit most often silently and even secretly, with the need to be loved and touched.

I was very tenderhearted and affectionate with the children at the center in Phoenix, and they flourished. The aides there told me that in the past, the kids would often cry when they'd get out of their parents' cars in the morning. Now they were leaping out of their cars, smiling, laughing, and running in to see us and get their welcome hugs.

To Learn and to Love

I emerged from those early years in teaching and social work with a philosophy of life that seemed awfully simple at the time, but to tell you the truth, it hasn't changed much for me in all the years since. In fact, it hasn't changed at all:

There are two things you're here to do on this earth: to gain wisdom, and to expand your capacity to love. *To learn and to love*: bottom line, those are really the only two issues that you need to be concerned about. Like I said, pretty simple.

The most important thing any of us could ever hear from another is "I love you." Here, I want you to do something for a moment; consider it a *thought experiment*. Think back to the last time you can remember someone telling you, "I love you." I hope it was in the last twenty-four hours, but even if it was weeks or months (or years?!) ago, think back to whenever that was and bring the feeling of it back up again. How did you feel when that person told you that?

Now, here's the experiment part: was that good enough to last you for the rest of your life? Or would you like to hear it again?

We don't ever complain about hearing that someone else loves us, do we? It just never gets old, does it? In fact, we gravitate to people who make us feel good about ourselves.

A few years after my time at the childhood development center, a book came out titled *Life after Life*, by Dr. Raymond Moody, with a foreword by Elisabeth Kubler-Ross (whom I interviewed on my television show, thanks to our mutual friend Dr. Gladys McGarey). Dr. Moody's book reported on the experiences of people who had been near death or even been pronounced clinically dead and then resuscitated (much like Editha Merrill). There have been many other such books since then, and they all report something similar: on the moments before death, your life passes before you.

I joked earlier about my near-death encounter when that plane dropped 10,000 feet in free-fall before the pilot regained control, but the truth is, I experienced something very similar to what these books all tell us. Here is what I saw, and what I strongly suspect everyone sees in such moments when you come face-to-face with your own imminent departure: every single incident in your life when you *could have* expressed love to someone, and you *didn't*—when you could have done something to make that other person feel better about themselves, and for whatever reason, you shied away from doing so.

As an adult, I developed the habit of always saying "I love you" before hanging up the phone. Then I shortened it to just, "Love ya!" Other people say, "Bye-bye," or, "Take care," or, "See ya." I say, "Love ya!" I mean, you never know. It might be the last time we ever talk.

I was on the phone once with the president of The Greyhound Corporation, discussing the possibility of doing some consulting work for them. As we finished up our call and were about to hang up I said, as I always do, "Love ya." And do you know, he called me back, acting as though he had forgotten something—but I had the feeling the man hadn't heard anyone say this to him in a while. And he sure isn't alone in that.

My kid brother Ray grew up to become a strong, burly police sergeant, not someone I would ever expect to say "Love ya" to his big sister. Besides his being a strong tough guy, crime fighter and all that, you know how siblings fight when they're young. We'd always been close, but still, "Love ya" was not our typical sibling-to-sibling conversation. When I started this end-of-phone-call habit, I wondered how it would land over on Ray's side of the line.

The first five or six times I said it to him, he didn't say anything back. Then one day, as we were just hanging up the phone, I heard him mumble, "Mmm hmm."

"Raymond," I said, "what did you just say? I'm sorry, I didn't catch it."

He said again, "*Mmm* hmm."

I said, "Ray, say it again, slowly—I still didn't quite understand you."

"Alright, doggone it!" he said. "*Love ya!*" And he quickly hung up.

After that, he always said "Love ya!" as he hung up the phone. His kids still do.

Chapter 6

BE YOURSELF ... EVERYONE ELSE IS ALREADY TAKEN

Toward the end of my second year of working at the child development center, something unexpected happened. I learned about a job opening at Arizona Public Service, the local utility company ... as a consumer service specialist. Yes, that's right: the very same job I'd failed to get back in Daytona Beach five years earlier. Which goes to show: don't give up on a goal, even when it looks like the goal may have given up on you.

In Florida I had been so convinced that I was qualified for that job, and so crushed when I didn't get it. For years afterward I'd thought I'd been turned down because they didn't think I was good enough, and I had continued to feel terrible about it. I had let the rejection make me feel inferior, and that feeling had seeped in through my pores and into my interior, working at my self-confidence like root rot on a houseplant with poor drainage. Even after learning that it'd had nothing to do with my actual qualifications and was based purely on the fact that I happened to be married, the residual awful feeling had not left me. Now this new opportunity offered me the chance to overcome that feeling once and for all. I wanted to prove to myself that I really *was* qualified.

I wanted that job so badly, and I prepared for it harder than anything I'd ever prepared for in my life. I went by the utility company office to see where I would be going for the interview the following day, so I would know exactly what it looked like ahead of time. I introduced myself to the receptionist. "I just wanted to make sure that I was familiar with the location," I said, "because I'll be coming in soon for a job interview here." By myself at home, I practiced walking into the room, practiced what I would say in the course of the interview, even practiced what I would wear. I can remember to this day exactly the clothes I had on during that job interview, because I had run through it in my head so many times that I had every detail of the experience memorized before it happened.

Back in Florida I'd been absolutely sure I *deserved* that job. This time, I wanted to make absolutely sure I was going to *get* that job. Twenty-eight candidates applied for the position; only one got it—and this time, thankfully, it was me.

Being rejected for that earlier job in Daytona Beach may have been one of the best things that ever happened to me, because that experience was what made me pursue this new job so completely—and it was what opened the door to everything that came later.

A Chance to Stretch and Grow

My new job at Arizona Public Service provided my first real opportunity to stretch my wings and develop the gift that I'd always felt was the reason I'd been put here in the first place. As I've said, I firmly believe that every single one of us is sent here with a gift to share with the world. Some are sent here to invent marvelous things, some are here to heal, some to lift our hearts with song or dance, or to tell stories. Some build buildings, some design computers, some play sports, some race horses. I stand up in front of people and talk.

I'd always been comfortable being up in front of other people, as you can probably tell from the stories of my school days. It was easy, when I was little. When you're young and innocent it's easier to pull off that brassy, show-must-go-on, put-me-up-there-I-can-do-anything spirit, to feel like that song in the musical *A Chorus Line*: "*I* can do that!" But by the time I reached adulthood I'd experienced enough crushing disappointments and failures to change the equation a little. Standing up in front of other people still came naturally, but exercising this gift also meant doing battle with such foes as self-doubt and lack of confidence, wounds to my ego and pride, and all the other ways we have of allowing the world to challenge our sense of self-worth. I'll bet you know what I mean.

It's a noble-sounding goal, to be yourself and nobody else. Of course, it's not as simple as it sounds. I've already described how helpful it was for me in social settings to embrace "being" a Miss Daisy in those moments when Miss Rita didn't have a clue what to do or how to act. And there were many others in my life who would serve as mentors, people I could emulate when I needed something to hold onto. I think we all learn, grow, and develop our sense of self in part by taking on the attributes and behaviors of those we gravitate to as mentors. But at some point you have to take off the training wheels and accept who you are, warts and all. That's one reason a sense of humor is so important: it helps smooth out the rough edge of those things we don't like about ourselves. (Erma Bombeck once told me, "It takes courage to laugh at yourself." It does—and it takes honesty, too.)

Oscar Wilde once wrote, "Be yourself; everyone else is already taken." The poet e.e. cummings put it this way:[10]

> To be nobody-but-yourself—in a world which is
> doing its best, night and day, to make you everybody
> else—means to fight the hardest battle which any
> human being can fight; and never stop fighting.

As far as I'm concerned, one of the best reasons to be nobody-but-yourself is that you'll only mess up trying to be anyone else.

It was in the course of my work at this new job I'd worked so hard to get, and especially in the course of what came on its heels, that I started to really get my feet under me and know that I didn't have to be perfect to feel comfortable and natural—that just being myself was good enough.

God Is Watching—Give Him a Good Show

The job at APS was quite varied, and it took me into all sorts of businesses and organizations large and small—even into a television studio. Not long after I started, I was invited as a representative of the utility company to appear on a television talk show on Channel 5, a local independent station, to demonstrate energy conservation, the use and care of appliances, how to use home lighting in decorating schemes, and things like that.

This was a new experience. I was no stranger to giving presentations, but I'd always been able to *see* the people I'd been there to train. Here, instead of a crowd of ten, or fifty, or five hundred faces looking back at me, there was this unblinking camera eye just sitting there staring at me. I had to remind myself that, behind that big owlish lens, there were hundreds of thousands of real live people sitting in their living rooms, dens, and kitchens, watching, listening, and taking it all in.

I suppose this could have been intimidating, but for some reason, it wasn't at all. It felt comfortable and natural. It was a hoot, owlish lens and all. After I'd been on television a few times and had a chance to do some cooking demonstrations, the show's producers realized that I really enjoyed cooking and wasn't bad at it, and I was having fun in front of the camera, so they gave me an eighteen-minute cooking segment.

I poured myself into this. I had learned something from my daddy that I never forgot: No matter what stage or station you are at in life, or where you are in any job, *do the best you possibly can.* Put your whole self into it. Be the best mechanic, the best housekeeper, the best department store mannequin, the best social worker, the best gas grill demonstrator you can possibly be.

I would learn this lesson again a few years later from Ted DeGrazia, the famous southwestern artist. Ted swore that when he first started out as a painter, he really wasn't very good. "Rita," he said, "if you do something long enough, you'll get good at it. And then people will tell others." Walt Disney put it this way: "Do what you do so well that they will want to see it and bring their friends."

A few years later I had the opportunity to met Mary Martin, the stage actress who played Peter Pan on Broadway for years. I could not imagine how she could act out this same story over and over, day after day, hundreds of times, and I asked her, "How do you keep it fresh? How do you keep up your enthusiasm for the role? How can you possibly make it so exciting, time after time? You've *got* to be tired of it!"

"Yes," she said, "I've done it hundreds of times. But I always remember, for that person in the audience, it's the first time they've ever seen *Peter Pan* live. If I were that audience member seeing it for the very first time, I'd want it to *feel* like the very first time—so that's how I do it."

Patricia Fripp, the executive speech coach, relates a story she heard from a client of hers, Sam Ross, the founder of Fantastic Sam's haircutting franchises. Sam had a special plaque on his wall with eight words that kept him inspired. "I'm not an especially religious person," Sam told her, "but having that plaque on the wall makes it a lot easier to make good business decisions."

The eight words were, "God Is Watching—Give Him a Good Show."

Well I don't know if God ever watched my cooking demonstrations, but I was determined to give my viewers in Phoenix the best show I possibly could. I put all I had into those little segments and did my darnedest to make every one of them fun and interesting for the viewers. In time, that effort would pay handsome dividends.

All You Can Control Is You

I had a friend at Arizona Public Service who also appeared on Channel 5 from time to time, and she had aspirations to work there full time. As it happened, the show's host was expected to retire within a few months, and it was no secret around the office that my friend had her eyes on that position. Her boss expected that she was going to get the job and routinely gave her time off to go down to the station and get to know the people there. In fact, we *all* thought she would get that job.

Sure enough, several months after I started working at APS, word went around that the host of *Open House* was retiring. What happened next, though, was not what any of us expected: the program director got in touch with me and said the studio wanted to offer *me* the job. My cooking segments had become quite popular; soon after I started doing them, people began writing in and saying they liked my jokes, my stories, and, yes, even my recipes. "Bring that Southern girl back on the show again," they said. So they had brought me back, and brought me back—and now they were inviting me to *host* the show.

I turned it down.

For one thing, I didn't think I could afford it: going from Arizona Public Service to Channel 5 would have meant a cut in salary. In truth, it was naïve of me to see it that way, because in television at the time the actual salary you made was only a small part of the equation, and it paled in comparison to what you could earn in commercials, endorsements, and other opportunities that came with the territory. But I didn't realize this at the time.

Finances aside, though, there was a more compelling reason to turn the job down: My friend really wanted that job more than I did. She had her heart set on it. She and I had been in graduate school together. She had given me a favorable recommendation for my job at Arizona Public Service, which had helped a lot.

I didn't mention my concerns about my friend at first and just cited the issue of salary as my reason for declining the offer. Soon the program director got in touch with me again and offered the job a second time, saying he'd match my current salary. I turned it down again. Finally he offered it a third time and said they would pay me a salary that was significantly *more* than I was currently making.

Now I felt I really had to explain myself and my concerns.

"Listen," I said, "I am truly honored at this generous offer. But I have to tell you, a friend of mine is expecting to get this job, and I think she's more qualified for it than I am. In good conscience, I can't take it because I'd be cutting her out of the opportunity."

"Rita," he said, "let me explain the situation. If you don't take this position, we do have someone else who will. She'd be our second choice, but she would be okay—and I'm sorry to say, but it's not your friend. I understand how you feel, but we are not going to be offering the job to her, regardless of your decision."

So I took the job.

I went to my friend, right away, and told her what had happened. "I told Fred that I felt you were more capable to do this job," I said, "that you had been around the station longer and you'd been groomed for it. The former hostess worked with you, and I felt that you were more qualified. And he told me that if I didn't take the job, it was going to be offered to someone else anyway. So I reluctantly accepted their offer—but I want you to know that I did *not* cut you out of this job."

My friend never spoke to me again.

It was a hard thing to get past. I never wanted her to feel bad; in fact, that was exactly why I had been so insistent about turning down the job in the first place. I don't ever want to make *anyone* feel bad about himself or herself—I mean, that's pretty much the opposite of my life purpose! But there was that business again about being in charge of the universe: fortunately or not, it's just not part of my job description—or yours, either.

You can't control what other people do, or how others will react to what you do. All you can control is what you do. It's such a simple truth, but so easy to forget, especially in the heat of the moment, and especially when someone you care about is suffering—and even worse, suffering because of something you've done.

But I had to let it go. There was nothing I could do to fix it. I knew I hadn't done my friend wrong, yet I felt terrible for her and was so sorry to see our friendship come to an end. At the same time, I had to accept the fact that I'd done all I could to make it right between us. That's all any of us can do.

The Deep End of the Pool

When I started at Channel 5 the show was called *Open House*. Soon it changed to *Phoenix at Midday*, and eventually changed again, becoming *Cooking with Rita*. We interviewed authors, celebrities, politicians, religious leaders, authors, prominent local businesspeople ... anybody who was anybody in Phoenix, visiting Phoenix, or traveling through Phoenix. The *Phoenix at Midday* show ran five days a week, an hour and a half a day—live. I had a newscaster who would give the news and a weathercaster who would tell us about the rain and sun, we had a chef come on and do cooking, we would have craft segments, and then we would do the interviews. Sometimes I even did the commercials myself, live and on the air. And I didn't just host the show—I also *produced* it.

Talk about being thrown into the deep end of the pool.

In terms of being on-camera and hosting a live show ninety minutes a day, five days a week, about the only training I had, if you can call it that, was the little cooking segments and guest appearances I'd been doing. But if I was unprepared as a broadcaster, I was even less prepared as a producer. For that, my professional background would have to be calculated as something on the order of *zilch*.

Not that it was all so terribly difficult. At least I didn't also have to serve the function of my own marketing and sales department, because by and large, celebrities would call *us* (or their PR staff would call us) and *ask* to be on the show, rather than my having to go chase them down. We got to more or less pick and choose.

And I loved, loved, *loved* doing those interviews. People fascinate me. And I think the more you accept yourself for who you are, the more it opens the door to accepting others for who *they* authentically are, too. Milton Berle, the much-beloved comedian, came on the show once and afterward he said something that meant a lot to me. "You know," he said, "you're either very good at this, or you really know how to fake it—because you seem genuinely interested in the people you interview. You treat everyone like they're special."

I so appreciated hearing that, because that was exactly what I strived to do.

And by and large, the guests were wonderful. I had an elderly man on the show one time who couldn't see or hear very well. I could see this wasn't going to be an easy interview. Before we started I said to him, "Sir, when we get near the end of the interview, I'm just going to sort of touch your leg, below the range of the camera, so you'll know we only have one minute left."

When we got to that point in the broadcast, I discreetly reached out and touched his leg—and he turned to me and said, "My dear lady, *why* do you have your hand on my leg?"

I was so tickled I just laughed and said, "Please excuse me, sir, I couldn't hold back."

Sometimes you just have to laugh and roll with the punches. Come to think of it, *most* of the time you just have to laugh and roll with the punches.

Trial by Fire

It might sound exciting, the idea of being a television talk show host. But here's the truth: when I was in television, the exposure put me in a position to get put down a *lot*. No matter who you are or how good you might be, nobody can please everyone. (And as John Wayne later said to me, "If you try to please everyone, you end up pleasing no one.") Can you imagine being broadcast into hundreds of thousands of homes? You can believe that not every person in every one of those homes had an altogether positive opinion of what they were watching. People love to nitpick, carp, criticize, and complain. Yes, my show was popular—and I also got a lot of negativity thrown at me.

Sometimes it even came from my guests.

A famous actor's brother, who was a gifted stage comedian and actor himself, appeared on the show once while he was in town to perform at a local comedy club. The interview was a disaster.

Most television talk show hosts spend some time with their guests before the show itself, getting to know them and covering some of the ground they might be talking about once they go on the air. But I had heard that Johnny Carson never pre-interviewed his guests, and that felt right to me: I wanted to make the experience feel fresh and spontaneous for the audience at home, and it seemed to me the best way to do that was to let it *be* fresh and spontaneous. So I adopted Johnny Carson's practice: while I did research my guests, I never pre-interviewed them.

Thus, when this comedian-actor and I sat down on the set to start our broadcast, it was the first time we had talked together.

He had had a long career on television and done a lot of fine work, but through no fault of his own, many of the shows he'd worked in were not that successful, and for years he had labored under the shadow of his extremely successful brother. As it happened, a few years *after* our interview he landed a plum role on a popular TV sitcom that finally earned him the success he deserved, but at the time this was still a few years away, and the shape his career had taken up to this point doubtless colored what happened next.

"It's great to have you on my show," I said. "You know, I'm surprised I've never met you before." Now, that's what I *said*—but apparently what he *thought* I said was, "I've never heard of you before," and he felt completely insulted by it. He must have thought I'd intentionally given him an awful slight, because he proceeded to go for my jugular and became confrontational with every question I asked. At the time (not yet realizing what had happened) I could not for the life of me understand what in the world he was being so mean about. All I could do was be myself and do my best to hobble through the next fifteen minutes. And let me tell you, they were fifteen long minutes.

Another time the award-winning actor Joseph Cotton (star of such classics as *Citizen Kane* and *The Third Man*) was in town to do some local theater and came on the show as a guest. When he showed up at the studio he'd brought along his wife, Patricia Medina, and he said he wanted her to go on the show with him. Patricia was an English actor with a significant film career of her own, but I didn't know her and honestly didn't really know any details about her career. I hadn't realized she was coming, so I hadn't done any research on her.

But I certainly couldn't refuse his request, so I said, "Fine, that's no problem. Now, I have not done any research on your wife. Can you help me out with that, so I can direct the questions appropriately and showcase her as well?"

"I'll handle that," he replied stiffly.

We got on the air—and Joseph Cotton said with biting sarcasm, "Well, Rita, I just wanted you to know how I met my wife. She was a hooker on the pier at Santa Monica."

I didn't know what to say. Obviously, the fact that I'd said I didn't know anything about her had offended him. What could I do? There was no "Take two" and starting over: we were broadcasting live. I did the only thing possible: I was as gracious as I could be and just let him continue taking his shots at me until that segment was over. He was downright nasty. It was one of the worst interviews I ever sat through.

Fifteen more of those incredibly long minutes.

After they left, onto the set walked my next guest, who happened to be Congressman John Rhodes, Sen. John McCain's predecessor and a good friend of Sen. Barry Goldwater. Congressman Rhodes had been waiting in the wings for his segment and had heard the whole thing with Joseph Cotton go down. After he got seated and we exchanged hellos, he turned half to me and half to the audience and said, "My dear, with what you just were exposed to, you are a demonstration of composure as I have never seen before. That was outrageous, how he talked to you."

Meanwhile (although I didn't know this until after the show) the studio switchboard had started lighting up like the Fourth of July. Our viewers were incensed. Evidently Mr. Cotton had not made any fans that day by belittling this young television hostess from Tennessee who was just trying to do her job and ask appropriate questions. I knew I was no match for an award-winning Hollywood actor, but hey, if you give people enough rope, they'll hang themselves.

The next day, I received a dozen roses—not from the actor, from the congressman, expressing his regrets for how I'd been treated by Mr. Cotton.

You can't control what other people are going to say, do, or think. You *can* do your best to take care of what *you* are going to say, do, and think.

"Tell Me Something Good About Me"

One day my boss called me into his office. He had a tendency in those days to come back from a two-martini lunch in a foul mood (a tendency he later turned around completely, I'm happy to say), and we would generally do our best to avoid him in the afternoons if we could. On this particular day, he had gotten mad about something I'd done, and he was fixing to ream me out about it.

What I'd done was harmless enough, or so I thought. One of the station's longtime employees had to have an expensive heart operation, and for some reason her insurance didn't cover all the costs, so I had organized a fund-raising dinner at a friend's restaurant to help generate the cash to help her pay for the surgery. My boss felt this made the station look bad because *they* weren't stepping in to pay for the operation. He thought I'd overstepped my bounds, and he was boiling hot about it.

Well, he cussed and stomped and chewed me out so bad it felt like verbal assault and battery. Now I have to admit, I am very tenderhearted and get emotional easily. My husband says my tear ducts are attached to my bladder, and that might be true. But after the bawling out I got that day, the tears were flowing. I was devastated.

What made it even worse was that right after he finished chewing me out, I had to go to the studio and face a TV camera. What's more, I had a speech to give that evening. I was supposed to talk for thirty minutes, but I had to stop after only seven minutes, excuse myself, and leave the stage. I kept hearing all the things he'd said playing in my head, and it made me completely choke. No matter how capable, experienced, or seasoned one may become, we are *all* vulnerable to having our confidence affected—and mine was shattered.

I had to do something.

The next day, I went to my boss's office, knocked on the door, and said, "Excuse me. Can I speak to you for a moment?"

I didn't think I had done anything wrong, but I didn't even try to get into any of that with him. Instead, I just told him how sorry I was that I had upset him (though I wasn't sorry about organizing the fund-raiser), and then I said, "But now, could you tell me something that's good about me? Because what you did to me yesterday has really messed with my confidence, and my job depends on my having confidence, especially when I'm on camera!"

He just looked at me. I don't think he was expecting me to say that, and he didn't seem to know how to respond.

So I kept talking. "As a matter of fact," I added, "your credibility's at stake here, because you are the one who hired me—and I don't want you looking stupid to the rest of the staff. So it might be a good idea right now to come up with a few good reasons you hired me for this job."

"Well," he said, and he took a breath as he thought for a moment. "You are certainly very personable, and you have integrity. You connect really well with people, and you do good interviews on the air. Well, obviously. I mean, yours is one of the highest rated local shows in Arizona."

I didn't say anything, just gave him a look that said, *And?*

"And, ah, you are hard-working, you have a great sense of humor, you don't take yourself too seriously. Lemme see...." He thought again for a moment, then added, "and you are charismatic, you are professional, and you are respected by your peers."

I smiled. "Why, thank you, Bill." I walked out of there feeling wonderful about myself and full of renewed confidence.

A week or two later, his secretary called one afternoon and said, "Rita, Bill's upset, and he's on his way down the hall to chew you out again. I know how sensitive you are, and thought you might want to get ready."

I got up from my desk and went out into the hallway to stand and wait for him with my arms folded in a *Bring it on!* posture. I saw him coming down the hallway, temples pulsating, fists tight, teeth clenched. Oh yeah, he was going to chew me out again, all right.

I start waving at him to come join me in my office, "Come on down! Come on down!" I could see his thinking shift as he walked toward me—because he knew that once he got through with what he had to say, I was going to turn around and say, "Now, tell me something good." Suddenly he stopped walking, looked over at me ... and then turned around and lumbered back up the hall to his office. He never did chew me out that day.

Over the years, he and I eventually became the best of friends.

Don't Give Away Your Power

When someone puts you down, you need to have some kind of defense in place so that you don't let it take down your self-confidence. Here's one response I've used that works really well: "No matter what you say or do to me, I'm still a worthwhile person." You can say this out loud, right to the person—if that works—or just think it to yourself. Either way is fine; the person who needs to hear this most is *you.*

"You're stupid!" *No matter what you say or do to me, I'm still a worthwhile person.*

"You're so lazy!" *No matter what you say or do to me, I'm still a worthwhile person.*

"You're no good!" *No matter what you say or do to me, I'm still a worthwhile person.*

"Fatty, fatty, two-by-four, can't get through the kitchen door!" *No matter what you say or do to me, I'm still a worthwhile person.*

No matter what others say to you or about you, it can't have any deep or lasting impact on you unless you let it. You can turn your power over to somebody else and give them the ability to affect your life in a negative way—and you can also choose not to do that. A dear friend of mine, John Addison, who is co-CEO of a publicly traded company and knows a thing or two about how to find good advice, says, "Never take advice from someone more messed up than you are." To which I'd add, never give *anyone* permission to make you feel bad about who you are—anyone including yourself. Because the truth is, however much others may say mean things to us, that typically pales in comparison with the negative things we tell ourselves about ourselves.

A big part of coming to the point of accepting yourself and learning to authentically *be* yourself is to quit running yourself down. It is amazing and appalling sometimes to realize just how much of what we tell ourselves about ourselves is negative. "You're fat, you're lazy, you're ugly, you're stupid, you're disorganized, you'll never be able to do this, you'll never amount to anything…" Often these are simply echoes of what influential people in our lives have said in the past that we believed and let inside our heads. I could have let the echoes of that tongue-lashing from my boss ricochet around inside my head for months. It's up to us to say, *No! I do not accept that opinion.*

The *New York Times* bestselling author Terry Cole-Whittaker wrote a book titled *What You Think of Me Is None of My Business*. That title says it all, doesn't it?

If the image you have of yourself is negative, then it's time to change it. It can help to actually sit down and write out a description of the person you would like to be. Make that description as detailed as you can: Is that person physically fit? Prosperous? Well-educated? Kind to others? Outgoing, friendly, enthusiastic, optimistic? Does that person have a particular ability or skill? Hey, this is your story you're writing, it's up to you. Write it out, keep it handy, and look at it from time to time to remind yourself of who it is you are in the process of becoming.

I also recommend reading Dr. Shad Helmstetter's classic, *What to Say When You Talk to Yourself*. This book and the concept behind it changed my life for the better, and its message is even more needed in today's world.

At the same time that you're creating a positive image of who you are *becoming*, also remember the person you have always *been* at your core, even since you were a baby.

Shortly after that day I was chewed out by my boss, I took out a baby picture of myself and put it on my desk. I highly recommend this. Here's what you do: Take a picture of yourself when you were a baby or toddler and put it on display on your desk in your cubicle or your office or wherever it is you spend your time. If anyone yells at you or treats you badly, show them the picture and say, "If this sweet little child were sitting right here in front of you, would you talk to her [or him] the way you just talked to me? Because this *is* me—and that's what you just did."

Knowing Erma

Soon after I began doing the show at Channel 5, Erma Bombeck, the enormously popular newspaper columnist and author of such bestsellers as *The Grass Is Always Greener Over the Septic Tank* and *If Life Is a Bowl of Cherries, What Am I Doing in the Pits?*, came on my show as a guest. I was a huge fan of Erma's and we connected immediately. Later on, when David and I moved to her neighborhood, we became neighbors as well, and in time she became one of my dearest friends, mentors, and role models.

One of the things I learned most from Erma had nothing to do with her amazing accomplishments or fabulous level of success, but with her complete and utter authenticity. Erma was exactly Erma, no more, no less, and no other.

Erma was so down-to-earth. She would call me for recipes, to ask who did my alterations, what florist did I use, or where was the best place to buy croissants. Family was always first with her. She loved to cook, and whenever David and I were invited over to have dinner with Erma and Bill it felt like an enormous privilege. She was an extremely private person, so much so that as famous as she was, hardly anyone really knew anything about her private life, which was exactly how she wanted it.

Erma once told me, "You know, Rita, being in television you live in a fishbowl. You get interviewed a lot. But here's the thing: you lose a lot of your power when everybody knows everything. That's why I'm so private about my life. Never tell everyone everything. Always have those personal, private parts of your life that you don't ever share with anyone. You'll never regret what you don't say."

Today, with Facebook, YouTube, Twitter, and all the social media we have, it seems to me that people are just opening their kimonos to the whole world. If Erma were here she would offer a word of warning: Careful—you might be telling people things you'll later really wish you hadn't told them. I loved my attorney friend Bettina Henry's advice regarding caution in communication when in conflict: "Never speak when you can nod; never write when you can telephone; and never, *ever* send an e-mail!"

In 1984, Erma was on the cover of *Time* magazine, and I asked her what that felt like. "Rita," she said, "if you do what you can do, with what you have to work with, you'll always feel good about yourself—and you'll feel as important as anybody on the cover of a magazine."

That was an illumination for me. That was when I began

to understand where low self-esteem comes from: it comes from comparing ourselves to Erma Bombeck, or to the models on the pages of fashion magazines, to our neighbor up the street, or the most popular kid in class.

When I was a little girl I always felt ashamed of the fact that my family was poor. As an adult, I came to realize that it wasn't the fact that we were poor that I had felt bad about. It was the fact that I was comparing myself to others who had more than we did. And there will always be someone richer, someone smarter, someone better-looking, someone more talented, more capable, more influential than you are. So what! You know what they will never be?

They will never be *you*.

Since that time, I've been on the cover of a number of magazines myself, and as exciting as it was at the time, I eventually had to admit to myself that at the end of the day, that magazine cover ends up lining the bottom of someone's birdcage. It's just not as big a deal as I thought it would be. Erma was so right. How you feel about yourself isn't dictated by whether or not you end up on the cover of *Time* magazine, or up on a stage, or lauded and praised by the world. How you feel about yourself is something that comes from inside yourself, and it is 100 percent up to you.

Erma didn't get on the cover of *Time* because she'd been part of any scandal, or found a cure for cancer, or been to the moon, or gotten elected to public office. She just made people laugh—and she was authentic.

Chapter 7

BIG PEOPLE, LITTLE
KINDNESSES

It's a funny thing about television. Imagine you're at a cocktail party and you've just gotten into conversation with someone you've never met before. They ask you what you do, and you say, "Well, I just received the Nobel Peace Prize, and I recently developed a cure for cancer, and believe it or not, I've been spending time in the Middle East and have established a surefire pathway for world peace ... and, oh yeah, I was in television for fifteen years." And you know what they'll say?

"Really? You were in *television*?! What was that like? Who did you work with?"

The power of the media. It's really kind of hilarious, and my boss was right: I never did take it too seriously. But I'll tell you what; I did get to do two things. I got the opportunity to touch a lot of lives. And I had the opportunity to rub elbows with an enormous number of highly successful people and learn an awful lot about who they are and what makes them tick. I did that show five days a week for fifteen years, and you can do the math: that's nearly four thousand shows' worth of interviewing anybody and everybody who came through town.

One of the first things I realized was that the more successful they were, the kinder they were. There's this idea floating around in our culture that the more successful people get, the snootier and more selfish they get. In my experience, nothing could be further from the truth.

To Whom Much Is Given

As I started interviewing celebrities, I quickly made it a regular practice to always make sure I got to know their handlers, whether that meant their agent or manager, hairdresser, makeup artist, chauffeur, or whoever. That's where you hear the best stories about these people and get to really learn who they are.

When Bill Cosby was coming on the show, I got to know his manager and heard a great story about him. It was around Christmastime and Bill was at a McDonald's in Manhattan, dressed down enough so that he wouldn't be immediately recognized. There was a Hispanic mother there, very pregnant, five little kids with her, all of them hungry. One of them said, "Ma, can we please have french fries along with our hamburgers? We're hungry!" It was clear that they wanted more to eat than she could provide.

Bill went up quietly to the far end of the counter and called one of the workers over. "Listen, my man," he said softly, handing the boy several bills, "I want you to take all those kids hamburgers, french fries, and milkshakes, and tell them Merry Christmas from Fat Albert." He also included a hundred-dollar bill for each of them, including one for the mother and one for the baby she was expecting.

Now I know that to a super-successful star like Bill Cosby, the cost of five burgers, fries, and milkshakes is an insignificant thing, and so is seven hundred in cash. But it wasn't insignificant to those five kids. Yes, it was easy for him to spend that kind of money—but it would have been just as easy not to. The point is, *he did*. That example has always meant so much to me. It exemplifies that little piece of wisdom that sounds so simple yet says so much:

> *To whom much is given, of him much shall*
> *be expected.*[11]

When you have the resources and you witness someone who doesn't, it means so much to them for you to step up and help. And it means at least as much to *you*. In fact, if you want to know the truth, you get even more out of the experience than they do.

A Date with the Duke

There was another reason I always like to go out of my way to get to know celebrities' handlers: these people are every bit as important as the ones who are in the limelight, and in many ways they can rightly take an important part of the credit for that limelight. Yet they are often invisible. A little acknowledgment and kindness can go a long way to making their day.

In my first few years of doing the show, one of the most exciting events was when I managed to get an interview with John Wayne, who was also a rancher in Arizona and typically visited the area over Thanksgiving. We had made arrangements with his business manager to meet the star at a certain time at his hotel to do the interview, but I've learned that just because these things are set up ahead of time doesn't necessarily mean they will happen when you get there. Sure enough, when I got to the Casa Grande hotel with my full crew in tow, with my boss's words ringing in my ears—him having pointed out that I was taking the crew out there on Thanksgiving, and it was costing us overtime, and nobody was happy about having to work on Thanksgiving, and after all this trouble I sure better get that interview—we couldn't find John Wayne.

We looked everywhere—the room where we were supposed to meet, the lobby, the various meetings rooms, everywhere we could think of. He wasn't there. I tried the number I had for him. No answer. I was frantic. No, I was way past frantic: I was downright *emotional*.

As it happened, the bellhop who was on duty was a fan of my local show and I had taken the time to be friendly and gracious toward him when we arrived at the hotel. "Don't worry, Miss Rita," he said, "I'll find John Wayne for you."

How would he do that? I wondered out loud.

"Easy. He rents the whole fourth floor," the bellhop said. He proceeded to call every single room on the fourth floor until he found the one he needed. He handed me the phone and he said, "Miss Rita, here's John Wayne."

And suddenly I was holding a telephone handset with John Wayne on the other end. I almost froze with fear.

"Oh Mr. Wayne," I gushed, "I've been looking everywhere for you, I have *got* to get this interview your partner promised, or I'm going to lose my job."

"Lady, calm down," he said. "Nobody told me about this interview. I'm watching a football game, but I'll be right there."

A few minutes later, in walked "the Duke" himself. You know how he always walked in the movies? That's the way he really walked. John Wayne was just exactly John Wayne— one of the most authentic people I ever met.

It was an interesting interview, because I was so nervous that he not only answered the questions, he also had to ask them. As he was removing his microphone, he said he looked forward to doing another interview sometime, and that hopefully the next time I wouldn't be so nervous and I'd be able to ask some questions, too. He smiled and winked at me, which made me feel better.

Predictably enough, after the interview a mob of people crowded around, hoping to get his autograph, which he graciously started giving. As he stood there signing things for people, he and I both noticed the bellhop striding over toward us with paper and pencil in hand. John Wayne reached over to take his paper and autograph it for him, but instead the bellhop reached over in front of John Wayne and held the piece of paper out to me. "No, Mr. Wayne, I'm sorry," he said, "I was hoping to get *Miss Rita's* autograph."

John Wayne turned and looked at me with astonishment and said, "Little lady, pardon me, but who in the hell *are* you?"

I had never felt so honored. And it was only because I had been nice to someone other people often didn't notice. It pays to be nicer than necessary. Besides, you meet the same people going down as you meet going up.

The next year it was a lot easier to get an interview with the Duke. He was still probably wondering who the heck I was.

Always Tip the Maid

I learned the importance of little kindnesses from my daddy, who never went past the third grade but from whom I learned more about life than from any college professor.

In all the years he drove me to school, from first grade right up through college, we never once passed a motorist with car trouble without Daddy pulling over to help them. It used to irritate me sometimes because it would make us late. "Daddy," I'd complain, "do you have to stop and help everybody who's got the hood up on their car?"

"Yes, I do," he would say, "because someday my babies might be on a highway with car trouble themselves, and somebody is going to stop and help them because we're stopping to help this feller right now."

Well, I've since been stuck on the highway with car trouble myself, and those people my daddy stopped to help were nowhere around! I'll say to myself, "Okay, now where are they, Daddy? You said they'd be here!" But you know what? Someone else *always* stopped, and when they did I'd say to myself, "Thank you, Daddy." What goes around truly does come around.

I've been teased at times because I tend to overtip. I've heard that's a sign of low self-esteem, but I've also heard it's a sign of high self-esteem, and I believe I'll go with that second interpretation. For me, more than anything else, it's an expression of understanding. When I see someone changing the sheets on my hotel bed, or parking my car, or taking my order and bringing me dinner, I know that for the grace of God that'd be *me* changing those sheets, or parking that car, or waiting on that table. And why in the world would anyone want to be rude to a waitress or waiter? (I'm especially kind to anyone who's going to be handling my food out of my sight!)

I am convinced that whatever successes I've had come about because of my commitment to living generously—especially when I didn't have all that much myself. Generosity may just be the most powerful force in the universe. People say *love* is the strongest force in the universe, and that's certainly true, too, because what is love if not generosity of spirit?

The benefit of accomplishment in my life is to be able to share it with other people. I know I can't feed all the hungry children in the world right now, but if I see someone around me who's hungry, I can sure help feed *them*.

My sister and I and our husbands were at a restaurant in Tennessee recently and noticed a soldier there in his camouflage fatigues, having dinner with his girlfriend. We asked our waiter to go over and let them know we would like to pay for their meal, out of gratitude for their service to our country.

Now, this was not an expensive place; a meal there probably doesn't cost more than $20. But when that soldier came over to our table to shake our hands, we could plainly see that he was pretty emotional. "I've never had anyone do anything like that for me before," he said.

"Well, it's about time they did!" we said. We never leave a restaurant that has a soldier, police officer, or firefighter dining without at least trying to pay for his or her meal.

A little later on the waiter came over and offered to give everyone at our table a glass of wine as his gift. That's the way generosity always works: when you give something, you *always* get back something that is even more than what you gave. A spirit of generosity always creates more of itself. Generosity is like love: it multiplies.

One time, when I was checking out of a hotel, I was

chased down the hallway by the woman who had just gone in to clean my room and found the tip I'd left. I don't remember what it was, but it certainly wasn't huge. She caught up with me and said, "I want you to know, because of what you just left me for a tip, my kids will have Christmas now." I felt ashamed that I hadn't left more.

Giving Kindness Brings You Kindness

Earlier I said the only way you can truly give love to others is if you first give it to yourself. But this also works the other way around. The more love you give to others, the more comes back to you, too—and not necessarily from those people you've gifted the most.

Whatever it is you're lacking in your life, start giving it. If you don't have enough love in your life, then start giving love. If you don't get enough praise, then give more praise. If you want standing ovations, then give standing ovations. If you want to be hugged, then give hugs.

And it truly *is* that simple. You're only going to get in life what you give away. The only thing you possess is that which you release.

If you want a rich life, then enrich the lives of others.

You don't have to be financially wealthy or have any more than you have right now to be a powerful philanthropist. *Philanthropy* is just a fancy pair of Greek words smushed together that simply means *loving people*. There are so many ways you can give and so many ways you can show love to others. Just look around in your environment and see who you can give a hug to, who you can encourage or support. It doesn't cost a lot of time or money, but each time that you interact with people you can leave them feeling better about themselves.

Edgar Cayce once said, "The way to heaven is on the arm of the man you help."

When I reach the end of my life, I don't want to feel that there were things I could have given that I never got around to. I want to feel that I have reached out and helped other people to the fullest extent that I was capable of doing. I want to be *used up*.

There's a saying I love: *Elephants don't bite, but mosquitoes and ants do*. It's the little things that we have to take care of and watch out for and be on top of, because they are really the most significant part of our lives. Your life isn't measured by grand gestures and earth-shaking events as much as it is by the little things you do—or don't do—every day.

Before I go to bed every night, there are two things I ask myself:

1) What did I learn today?

2) What did I do today to help someone else?

If you want to have a good night's sleep and wake up feeling good about yourself, start taking a moment to ask yourself those two questions every night. You are your destiny; what you think about today is what you'll become tomorrow. If you start planting those two questions in your mind, those seeds of greatness, in time you will harvest their fruit.

Out of the Blue

I read in the paper a story about a woman and her five children who had been turned away from a shelter for battered women and children. As much as they wanted to take her in, they were already jammed to the gunnels and just couldn't take another body into their building. In fact, they were in the middle of urgently seeking more funds so they could enlarge their facility. Their office was only a double-wide trailer.

The women turned around and went back home. When her husband found out where she had gone to try to get help, he grabbed a pair of scissors and stabbed her to death, right in front of their children.

When I heard this, it made me absolutely heartsick. The idea that there was this wonderful place staffed by people who were qualified to help and desperately wanted to help but who couldn't, simply because they didn't have the physical space ... this was something I just could not abide. But what could I do? I didn't have the extra cash to give them myself, and with my plate so ridiculously full I didn't see how I could possibly put in the time to organize and spearhead a major fund-raising effort.

Maybe you've heard that we often get our best ideas when we're in an environment with lots of negative ions, like out in the country, at a mountain lake, or by the seashore. For me, it's generally when I'm shaving my legs in the bathtub. I'm guessing God figures this is the only time I'm sitting still in one place long enough to listen.

So I was in the aforementioned sanctified place one night, shaving away, and the thought came into my head: *You have to raise $150,000 for the Sojourner Center*. No burning bush, no voice of thunder, and no wondrous signs. Just me, my Lady Remington, and that impossible thought plunked right down in the middle of my head.

Oh, Lord, I thought. How on earth am I going to do that—you know how busy I am!

Then I got to thinking. I'd helped a lot of people over the years, sometimes just by virtue of having them as a guest on the show. For example, there was a retired firefighter who had invested everything he had into creating a little paint store that had not done well and was on the verge of closure. I heard about his situation and invited him onto the show to demonstrate faux painting. He told us that the day before he was on the show, he had sold a total of one paintbrush. He was about to shutter the store and go out of business. When he opened up the morning after our show, there was a line of customers waiting, and he was able to keep his doors open after all.

I decided to squeeze a little time out of my days to start calling people, and keep calling until I'd found 150 people who would each contribute $1,000. That shouldn't take long, right?

Ha. I pretty quickly found out how well *that* idea

worked. Soon it felt like it would be easier to get 1,500 people to give me $100 each … or maybe get 150,000 to each give me a dollar. Days went by and I wasn't getting anywhere. I didn't see how on earth I was ever going to get that $150,000 together—but I *had* to.

And then, out of the blue, the man who had owned the failing paint store called.

"I heard you were raising money for the Sojourner Center," he said. I have no idea how he'd heard this. He was not on the list of those I'd called; that list had been limited to people whom I knew were quite well off. But here he was, on my phone. "Rita," he said, "I don't think I've ever thanked you enough for having me on your show. You may not realize just what an impact that one day had."

No, I admitted, I really didn't. I knew he'd been able to keep his store open, and I was thrilled about that. But that's about as far as I knew the story.

"Well let me tell you the rest," he said. "Today my little paint store is worth eight million dollars. I am a wealthy man because you invited me to be on your show and you showcased my business. I want you to know I'm putting a check in the mail to you today, and I hope you'll accept it."

He sent me a check for $15,000, and when word got around it got the ball rolling. My dear assistant Tami Taase set up a chart in our office that looked like a giant thermometer to measure donations, with a goal at the top of $150,000. Before long, I had the full amount I was called to raise. (Since then, from fundraisers, family, friends, and colleagues, our donations have grown to over a million dollars. Sojourner now offers shelter to hundreds of domestic-violence victims and their children on two campuses in Arizona. The need is still great, though, since domestic violence is an epidemic affecting over 25 percent of our population. You can find their website at www.sojournercenter.org.)

When you do for others, you *will* get a return. You won't necessarily know where it's going to come from, or how— but I promise you, it *will* come.

Someone Who Believed in Me

It was through a series of little kindnesses that the next chapter in my career opened up.

A few years before joining the show at Channel 5, when I was still working for Arizona Public Service in the sales department, I was tasked with getting a speaker for a big event that was coming up. There was a well-known speaker in town by the name of Cavett Robert; I had heard him and thought he was amazing.

Cavett was the first major public speaker I got to know. Before I knew Zig Ziglar, before Og Mandino, before my dear friend and mentor Joe Larson, Cavett was my first mentor in the arena of public speaking.

I knew that Cavett lived right here in Phoenix, so I hired him to come and speak for our event. His speech was an absolute hit. But it created a huge dilemma for me—because I had to speak right after him. What was worse, he'd just said everything I'd planned to say.

When I'd first heard him speak, I was so impressed that I had memorized everything he said. What I didn't know was that a lot of great speakers really only have one speech. They may adjust and tailor it to fit the audience they're with, but it's still essentially the same speech. I had memorized Cavett's speech, because I thought it was so good, and that was pretty much what I planned to deliver myself. But as I listened to him now, I realized with horror that he was giving that same speech all over again! "Holy moly," I thought, "he just gave my speech!"

What was I going to do? I had to punt. To this day I can't tell you what I talked about, but somehow I pulled something out of my head and managed to make it through.

Afterward Cavett came up to me and said, "You know, you have a gift for speaking. You've got humor, and you've got timing, and you have an ability to interact with the audience. You have stage presence. You could be a very successful public speaker."

This made a huge impression on me. Giving cooking demonstrations was one thing; being a guest on a television show was another. But standing up on a stage in front of thousands of people, with no props, no kitchen, no banter back and forth, just me talking, holding everyone's attention and keeping that thread going for twenty minutes, forty minutes, up to an hour or even more? I had never seen myself doing *that*. In fact, I was in awe of Cavett and anyone else who could do such a thing.

When I was in eighth grade, I was elected president of Central Junior High School, which meant it was my job to facilitate our assemblies. I can still remember being so nervous that my knees literally knocked together as I introduced guest speakers in front of an audience of eight hundred kids.

But if Cavett said I could do it, maybe I could. That little kindness he showed me that day, letting me know he believed in me, was the catalyst that launched a whole new career, one that in the years to come would take me hundreds of thousands of miles around the world meeting and having an impact on hundreds of thousands of people.

With even the smallest gesture of faith, belief, or acknowledgement, we each have an enormous power to influence others positively. When I was young, I had set a goal, which is defined as a predetermined idea directed toward a desired result, to impact the world. I had no idea how, but the *how* always comes to you when you're clear on the *what and why*.

The great irony of that pivotal conversation with Cavett Robert was that I was far from the only person he ever said this to. Later on, after I'd already become an experienced speaker and gotten to know Cavett, I realized that he said much the same thing to *everyone*—bellhops, taxi drivers, skycaps, flight attendants. We'd go out for lunch or coffee with a few of our speaker friends and Cavett would tell the waitress, "You know, you ought not to be a waitress. You ought to be a public speaker." We would all look at each other and roll our eyes. Many of us were there because he had told us the same thing, and we were gullible enough to believe him. This included some pretty famous speakers whose names you would recognize. Of course, I didn't know any of this at the time, and I was naïve enough to believe him.

Cavett was a con artist—but a very special, magical kind of con artist. He could con you into thinking you could do more than you really could. And the magic of it was, if you kept believing it, then in time *you could*. Did he really see me as a speaker, that day I stood up on the stage and stumbled around trying to figure out what in the world I was going to say after the speech he'd just given? Or was he just doing what he always did, sharing the generosity of his enormous belief in people more or less indiscriminately? I'll never know, and I suppose it doesn't matter. He told me he believed in me, and it was contagious, because in time, I did too.

Raising the Bar

When I did finally get into public speaking as a career, it was out of economic necessity. As I had feared when I originally turned down the job offer at Channel 5, I was not earning that much money in local television. My elderly parents needed assistance, and my brother Ray had been diagnosed with lymphoma. My sister Euphiazene was making less than $100 per week and her husband was disabled after having two open heart surgeries. I needed to generate more income!

However, at first I really had no idea that public speaking could be a viable income source. It more or less came with the territory of being a television personality, so as the years went on I began giving little talks more and more, but I wasn't charging a fee for these little speeches. I was representing the station and just regarded this as a normal PR sort of activity.

Cavett had boosted my self-confidence as a speaker, but it still hadn't sunk in yet that I could make a *living* doing this.

Then one day I spoke at a huge charity event for the local hospital auxiliary, and they had Congresswoman Bella Abzug, the famous feminist leader, on the same program. My talk got a standing ovation—but Bella Abzug was not well received. This is a very conservative town. I hadn't heard her speak before and I didn't really know much about her, but it didn't take long to realize that her talk was going over like the proverbial lead balloon. In our audience of about two thousand there were people actually groaning out loud and even booing. It was awful.

After the program was over, the woman who had organized it came up to me and said, "Oh my God, Rita, I am so sorry."

"Sorry?" I said. "Why? I thought I did pretty good."

"Oh, no," she said, "you were fine. But Ms. Abzug—we flew her in first class and paid her a $5,000 honorarium, and she didn't even get any applause! You were the best thing on the program. You saved the day."

I smiled and thanked her—but what I was thinking was, "Five thousand dollars?! You mean, I could get *paid* for doing this?" I had done my talk for free. As a matter of fact, at that point I did *all* my talks for free, or for a tiny honorarium (which I donated to one of my favorite charities) that was so close to nothing that it might as well have been free. Clearly, it was time for this to change. I needed to start charging for what I was doing.

This was a big moment in my career, because it meant confronting my own sense of self-worth in a very concrete, measurable way. "Rita," I told myself, "if you speak for nothing, then you are saying that you are *worth* nothing. And that's just not true."

If you write for nothing, teach for nothing, consult for nothing, work for nothing, then you're saying you are worth nothing. You're saying you don't deserve to be paid. And you *do* deserve to be paid—that is, you deserve it if you make yourself worth it.

From that moment on, I raised the bar of expectation for myself. And something remarkable happened. As I began charging more, clients began respecting me more. Word began to spread, and I started being invited to give talks outside of Phoenix.

I continued doing speeches for free for nonprofits, and

they constituted a significant portion of the talks I did. And in truth, even when I did one of those I would invariably wind up getting another paid speech out of it, because somebody in the audience would book me later for another event. But other than actual charities, I stopped speaking for pennies. I soon found that I really enjoyed doing this, and at the same time, that I could make a genuine difference in people's lives. And more the marvel—I was generating needed income to help support my family in Tennessee.

Fear of Speaking

David Wallechinsky, author of *The Book of Lists*, once told me that speaking in front of an audience was the number one fear in the world. "Really!" I said. "What's number two?" "Death by fire," he replied. I was almost afraid to ask what number three was, but I did, and he said, "Death by cancer."

Well, that puts things in perspective. Every time I stood up to give a speech, I couldn't help thinking, *most people would rather burn to death or get cancer than do what I'm doing right now.*

At first I would get terrified whenever I had to give a speech. Then I read about some research that'd been done on speakers and their audiences. It found that out of your average audience, 10 percent don't listen because they're worrying about something. Another 10 percent don't listen because they came with someone else, and aren't really interested themselves. About 47 percent have enough interest to listen, and the remaining 33 percent are having sexual fantasies.

I figured, okay, we're all going to have a good time no matter *what* I say. After that I didn't get quite as nervous.

One thing that has always helped calm my nerves on the stage, of course, has been remembering to hang onto my sense of humor, and to insert it whenever possible. (I've also heard that when people laugh while they're listening, their retention increases by as much as 87 percent.)

When I give a speech, I don't usually have a structured

outline. (I have more than thirty hours of internalized material, and generally draw on it extemporaneously as I go.) I never use PowerPoint or any kind of slides (unless it is a more extended, lengthy seminar, where visuals become much more important). I used to play a joke on the audiovisual crew. I'd go onstage after being introduced, stand up there in front of 5,000 or 10,000 people, and say, "Okay, now just to get started, if we can please show the first PowerPoint?"

Everything would get very quiet and I could hear people scrambling backstage in harsh whispers going, "Where's her PowerPoints?! She didn't *give* me any PowerPoints! Did she give *you* any PowerPoints?!"

Then I'd say to the audience, "Just kidding—I don't actually have any PowerPoints. I'm just messin' with the crew backstage. Can you hear 'em all running around back there?"

I've done that often enough that they're on to me now, and if I try it today, there aren't as many heart attacks backstage. Now they just laugh at me.

Along with a sense of humor, one essential element in being able to speak in public is to retain a sense of humility. No matter how much you practice, you're never going to get it perfect, and the sooner you make peace with that and accept your imperfection, the sooner you can get on with it and start doing a pretty decent job. Besides, every speech is like a marriage: you don't really know what it's like until you get into it.

I have read one of the characteristics that distinguishes man from lower animals is that only man can stand upright before a crowd and put both feet in his mouth. Well, this is also true of woman.

I was to make a presentation and introduce Marion, a close friend of mine, to a group of two hundred salesmen. Before the presentation, Marion confided to me she was very self-conscious because the audience was made up entirely of men. I could not for the life of me understand this. She was articulate, beautiful, talented ... what was the worry?

"Marion," I said, "what could you possibly feel self-conscious about? Just because the audience is made up of men is no reason to think they won't respect you and listen to you. You're amazing!"

And she said, "Well, it's because of the size of my breasts."

Now that had not occurred to me. This was not a problem I'd ever suffered with. But even if I'd never been in Marion's shoes (if you know what I mean) I could still sympathize, and I immediately saw her point: she's quite voluptuous. Still, I didn't think that was any reason for her to be nervous.

"Marion," I said, "that's just silly. You're so savvy and articulate; you just get up and do the best job you can. Nobody's going to be thinking about the size of your breasts."

She seemed somewhat reassured, but I could tell she was still a little on edge.

The time came, and I stood up to introduce her. I gave a brief summary of her background and credentials, and concluded with this:

"… It is indeed a pleasure to present to you today, my *very breast friend*."

Oops. My Freudian slip was showing. I blew it. The audience went nuts. Sorry about that, Marion.

The Currency of Kindness

While it was Cavett's little kindness that first convinced me I could become a speaker, it was his assistant Merlyn Cundiff who taught me that kindness is a currency that can be invested, circulated, and multiplied.

Merlyn was a very astute businessperson. While there were a number of people pivotally involved, it was really Merlyn who was the driving force of an idea that in time would change the public speaking industry. Soon after I met the two of them, Cavett and Merlyn spearheaded an effort to create an organization for public speakers. Before long a bunch of us were sitting together one day on someone's patio in Phoenix, each of us writing out a check for $250, and that was the seed money that started what became the National Speakers Association. Two hundred and fifty dollars seemed like an awful lot of money to me at the time, but it was worth it. Today the NSA has thousands of members and more than forty chapters around the country.

Merlyn mentored me when I was just starting out and gave me invaluable feedback. At one point she invited me to come work with her: Cavett and I would be the speakers, and she would be our agent. I thought this was a great idea and signed a contract with her, but she said, "Before I countersign this and we make it official, I want you to think about it for twenty-four hours."

I thought about it hard. As part of the terms of our agreement, she wanted me to commit to speaking at least fifteen days a month. The more I turned the idea over in my head, the more I realized it was just too much. I wanted to start a family, and I was concerned that being gone that much would have a negative impact on my marriage. How could I commit to at least fifteen days out of every month on the road? Before the twenty-four hours was up I called her back and told her that I was flattered, but I couldn't do it. I am so grateful that she had the insight and graciousness to make sure I took the time to think this through.

When we were in the middle of discussing this potential partnership, Merlyn gave me a ring, a 14k gold band with two hands clasped together. "It's a sign of support, friendship, and appreciation," she said. "It's a *people-builder's ring*. I want you to wear it as a reminder that someone is always with you; that when you succeed, I succeed; and when you suffer disappointments, I'm right there, feeling your disappointment."

"Merlyn," I said, "I don't know how I can accept such a generous gift. How can I ever repay you?"

"Well," she replied, "I was actually hoping you would ask that. If you accept this, here's what I want you to do: I want you to promise me that you'll do the same thing for at least one other person."

I still have that ring, and wear it on my pinky finger. And

I have since awarded thousands of identical rings to other people whom I believe in.

A Kindness Out of the Blue

Another person who invested the currency of kindness in me was Og Mandino. Og was a good friend as well as a mentor who encouraged me and believed in me.

In 1977, when I had just been speaking for a few years, the National Speakers Association established a lifetime award called the CPAE Speaker Hall of Fame to honor outstanding professionals in the field. (CPAE stands for Council of Peers Award for Excellence.) A few years later, Og nominated me for the award. There was some resistance to my getting it (politics and personalities: alive and well wherever people congregate!) and the nomination died. The next year, he nominated me again, and the following year, and the following year yet again. I had become the Susan Lucci of professional speakers! (Leading lady on the daytime soap *All My Children*, Susan was nominated twenty-times for an Emmy award before she finally won one.) In 1994, I finally won the coveted CPAE Speakers Hall of Fame award. It was one of the proudest accomplishments of my career, and it would likely never have happened if not for the constancy of Og's support.

Whenever another speaker is nominated for the CPAE, someone is selected to speak at the ceremony and tell the audience all about the recipient. When I won, it was Og who gave my introduction.

By any measure, Og Mandino has inspired more people than just about any other nonfiction author you can name. One of his books, *The Greatest Salesman in the World*, is one of the bestselling nonfiction books of all time. All told, his books have sold more than 50 million copies and have uplifted and inspired the lives of millions of people.

Og was extraordinarily gifted, and his gift was of an almost otherworldly sort. Whenever he was engaged in writing a book, it was as if he would become an entirely different person: he ate differently, slept differently, talked differently, and his personality became different. It was like he was taken over by a higher power. Yet when you were around him at other times, he was just a normal person who never took himself very seriously. Og was completely beloved by everyone who knew him. He was also a devoted friend. For years and years, we would get together with Og and his wife, Bette, every Christmas season at our friend Helen Anderson's house and have a party. Og would always dress up as an elf, with a green felt hat and green shoes with bells on the ends. He cracked us up every year without fail.

I sometimes talk about how people become bigger than themselves by sharing their gifts with the world. Og was the biggest of people.

He called me one day in October 1996 when I was out and left a message on my answering machine. "Rita, it's Og. I was just thinking about you. I know how busy you are, I just want to tell you how much your friendship has always meant to me. I just wanted to take the time to let you know that." And he went on and said a few more very nice things, then said goodbye and hung up.

Now, he had no real reason to do that. It was such a sweet message.

The next day while doing some work around the house, he fell off a ladder and hit his head. His wife, Bette, insisted that they go to the hospital. He seemed okay, and they sent him home. As it turned out, he was not okay; he was bleeding internally. The next morning, he died.

I have always regretted that I did not have the chance to call him back, thank him for his sweet message, and tell him how much he meant to me, too. At the same time, I have also always been so grateful that he followed whatever impulse led him to pick up the phone that day and call, out of the blue, for no reason at all, just to let me know he was thinking of me.

Out of the blue. For no reason at all ... except that it just occurred to him.

What better reason could there be to share a little kindness and tell someone we love them?

Chapter 8

LAUGH YOUR WAY
TO SUCCESS

(OR, HOW TO COPE WITH STRESS, GUILT, CHANGE, FAILURE, AND LIFE'S OTHER LITTLE BLESSINGS)

I was doing a two-day workshop in Washington, D.C., for the National Security Agency, when someone came out and told me my husband was on the phone for me. Scared me half to death. I went running to the phone, picked it up, and spoke into it breathlessly. "Hello?!"

I heard my husband's voice say, "Rita? This is David."

"Yes," I said. "After twenty-five years of marriage, I recognize the voice."

"Rita," he said, "I don't have any clean underwear."

I took a breath and felt my heartbeat slow to normal.

"David," I said, "you were one of the smartest guys I

ever dated. You graduated from Vanderbilt with honors. I couldn't have even gotten *into* Vanderbilt. You have a master's degree from ASU with honors. You got an invitation to join Mensa." I paused. He didn't say anything. I continued, "You know, I thought I married somebody smart enough to know that he could turn those things wrong-side-out and wear them another week."

You Have to Bring Humor to the Table

I mentioned earlier that you have to have a good sense of humor to keep a marriage alive. I learned this early on from my parents.

My daddy came to the table one Sunday afternoon after he got home from work. He was working two jobs, six and a half days a week, and he'd also been out cutting grass. He was sweaty and hot, and he didn't have on his shirt.

Mama said, nicely, "Jimmy, go put your shirt on."

He said, "I'm in my own home. We don't have any company. I'm not putting my shirt on. I'm comfortable just like this."

She said, "Jimmy, I cooked a nice dinner. I don't want to sit here and look at your hairy, sweaty chest while I'm trying to eat my dinner."

He said, "I don't care what you say, I'm not putting my shirt on." (That's not the full quote; he added a few more colorful words in there too.)

She said, "Fine." She excused herself from the table. After a minute she came back into the room stripped to the waist, sat down, and said, "Well, now we'll all be comfortable." Daddy never came to the table without his shirt on again.

Here are the two things I learned from that: First, you need to set boundaries for how you are willing to be treated. And second, if you want a relationship to last, you've got to bring a sense of humor to the table. So to speak.

Ladies, let me tell you something: before you marry a man, you don't know how loud he can eat an apple. (Answer: loud enough that you can hear it from four miles away.) You don't know he's going to get up at 4:30 a.m. to dig into a bowl of cereal before he goes out to play golf, and you can hear it all over the house. Before you marry a man, you do not know that he has gas. Twenty, thirty, forty years later you find yourself thinking, Man, it must have been backed up to his ears, because all these years later it's *still* coming out. (I have also learned that gas is contagious.)

I often tell women, "If you've got a good husband, keep him, because they're so hard to train." And I don't know about you, but I don't have the same equipment to train with I used to. If you've got a good husband, tell him you love him before another woman does. Because for every woman with a headache, there's another one with aspirin in her pocket.

Laughing is internal jogging. It causes the muscles around the face to vibrate, which causes blood to rush to that area, which in turn improves brain function. You think better and you feel better, and your health is improved. As it says in Proverbs, "A joyful heart is good medicine."[12] Besides, if you hold those chuckles back, the air tends to go back down and expand the hips!

David usually picks me up at the airport at the end of one of my trips, and I so appreciate it. For years I've done an awful lot of flying around the country, and it always meant so much to me to know that once I got to the curb, all I had to do was find David's white car and climb in, and my trip was over.

One time I ran out onto the curb with my carry-on suitcase (there are only two kinds of luggage: carry-on and *lost*) and right away saw his big white SUV. I stepped to the back door, opened it and quickly hurled my suitcase inside, then pulled open the front passenger-side door and jumped into the front seat. The man behind the wheel looked at me and said, "Well, where are we going?" He was not my husband.

"Oh, I'm so sorry," I said as I climbed out of the car and hauled my suitcase out of the back seat. Hey, all white SUVs look the same to me.

I was so glad that man had a sense of humor.

Thank You for Not Smoking

One reason I think we're meant to get through life with a sense of humor is that the Bible says we were made in God's image, and if God doesn't have a sense of humor, I don't know who does.

I'll give you an example.

In the summer of 1996, our whole family went up to the mountains for the Fourth of July weekend, taking our dog Chelsea with us. That night there was a terrible storm and lightning struck the house. It caught fire and burned all night in the rain. When we came home the next day it was a smoking, smoldering wreck. Our friend Bill Bombeck had to loan us a car, because our other car was torched—it had exploded in the garage. I'm still grateful to Bill for showing up at our house with sandwiches and soft drinks. The firemen had pulled all our furniture out onto the front yard. It looked bizarre, as if someone were holding a yard sale in a war zone. I realize it was all just stuff, and stuff is not what our lives are about. All our worldly possessions are just on loan, anyway, and we're going to get rid of it all eventually. I've never seen a hearse with a U-Haul behind it. But still, when it was all over we had lost everything, much of it due to smoke damage. We weren't able to move back in until two years later.

The interesting thing about all this was that, after twenty-eight years, I had wanted a new house, and had even gone out looking at homes. But David was perfectly happy with where we were and saw no reason to move. So God burned the house down and gave us both what we wanted: After two years of repair and remodeling, I got a new house, and my husband didn't have to move.

The reason I feel confident this was God's doing is that he left a calling card. The entire time we had lived there I had a sign hung over our front door, engraved in brass, that said,

The Davenports thank you for not smoking.

So what did we get? An entire *house* that smoked! Hey, nobody has a better sense of humor than God.

Laughing through Parenthood

In my thirties, I was told I could not get pregnant and would never have any children. In fact, my doctor advised me to get a hysterectomy. Like most things I was told I couldn't do, this one turned out not to be true. (As I found out later, many hysterectomies are not needed at all.) And as with most things I was told I couldn't do, I went right out and got a second opinion.

The second-opinion doctor told me, "What?! Why in the world would anyone recommend a hysterectomy? There's nothing wrong with you! You have a slightly tipped uterus, that's all. Of course you can have children."

And I did. In 1978 I gave birth to a boy, whom we named Michael. The experience of childbirth confirmed my long-held suspicion that God is indeed a man. I was in labor with Michael for thirty-two hours. I'm sorry, let me be more specific: thirty-two *long* hours. No woman would have done that to another woman.

Now I know some women object to the story that God created man first, but to me, it makes a lot of sense: He was practicing. It's like when you make pancakes, there has to be a first pancake, because you need to sort of test the process out, see where the flaws are, so you can adjust the heat and correct your mistakes with the next try. And once you've made it, you might not serve it on a plate, but there's no point throwing it out, right?

I'm kidding. I love men. (Especially short men, because they can't see your roots.) I even married one, and we produced two more of them.

My husband David says that God started with man because He didn't want to have to listen to a lot of suggestions. Now, I don't know about you, but I'd have had a few. For one thing, why didn't He let us all stand up to go to the bathroom? There wasn't anything wrong with that arrangement.

I wondered about that when I was a little girl, and my mama, of course, had an answer: "Because He knew that was the only time a woman would get to sit down."

Two years later, Michael's little brother Scott was born.

One reason I talk about how important it is to develop a sense of humor is that it is something none of us are born with. I know this from experience: I have given birth twice and distinctly remember that neither baby was laughing when he came out. Come to think of it, neither was their mama.

In any case, now I was a broadcaster, a producer, a speaker, a wife, *and* a mother of two sons. As I like to say, I now had an heir and a spare.

Earlier I said "getting married is easy—*staying* married is the challenge." The same thing applies to having children. Having them is easy; raising them is a whole other story, and it takes putting your whole self into it to do it anywhere even close to as well as they deserve.

That, and an ever-ready capacity to laugh when your impulse is to cry or scream.

One time we were preparing to go on a vacation, had the van all packed up and everything, when we suddenly realized the boys weren't there. We went to look for them and couldn't find them anywhere. They had disappeared. They were four and six years old. For the next hour, we searched everywhere. Finally we found them. They were giggling and hiding in the shower. They thought it was funny. We were not able to see the humor in it, though we tried.

As much as I am an advocate of positive thinking, I have to admit that I still have negative thoughts at times. But I *never* had such negative thoughts in my entire life as I started having after the boys came along. I never imagined how creative I truly was until I started seeing some of the negative thoughts I could come up with.

Driving to work one morning, I heard a news report about tarantula eggs being found in some produce in the Phoenix area. I started thinking about the lunch I had packed Michael for school that morning, and it occurred to me that

I had put a banana in his lunchbox. I got to thinking, "You reckon there could be tarantula eggs in that banana? Naw... probably not. But what if there are?"

Real quick, I did a U-turn and headed back toward our neighborhood, whipped by the school, parked my car out in front and tore in there, high heels wobbling on the pavement as I ran, just to check it out. No, as far as I could see there weren't any tarantula eggs in the banana. I wobbled back to my car and made it to work on time, feeling much better now. Poor teacher's probably still shaking her head.

And that wasn't the only teacher who must have wondered about that Mrs. Davenport. During second grade show-and-tell one day the students were each asked to share what their mother did, if she worked outside the home. Michael stood up and told the class, "My mother works conventions and gets paid by the hour!" I know this only because the teacher called me later that day laughing and suggested that I might want to explain to Michael a little more about my career as a speaker.

I am not only a big fan of humor in general, but I also happen to believe, as I mentioned, that nobody has a better sense of humor than God, and I offer the following story as proof.

I've told you about how I saved up to buy my first Waterford crystal glasses when I was in my twenties, and how I came to such an appreciation for Waterford crystal. If you haven't already suspected this, let me tell you: that was just a setup for another cosmic joke. One day when I had taken the boys with me on a shopping trip, Scott knocked over a display in the department store while reaching for a candy dish full of jelly beans. And yes, you have already guessed correctly: it was a display of Waterford crystal.

Very funny, God.

Happily, although the entire display came down, not a single item broke. (God was just messing with me.) Trying to stay calm, I stooped down to get at eye level with Scott, while all the salespeople and customers watched to see what I would do, and simply told him, without any yelling or spanking (hey, we were *both* traumatized!), that he had made an unwise choice. After that episode, he was more careful and understood the consequences of his choices.

I made both boys take piano because I'd heard that this would boost their intellectual capabilities, and besides, I'd always wished that I could have taken piano. They hated it. After three years I finally let them quit, but only after they told me that if I didn't, when I got old, they were going to put me in a nursing home in a room without any windows.

One day, when my boys were both in their teens, I read an article on the front page of *USA Today* that said the intelligence of female children is determined predominantly by the father, and the intelligence of male children is largely dictated by their mother. I read this item out loud to the boys and then added, "Well how do you like that? Your intelligence is determined by me!"

Scott looked over at Michael and said, "We're screwed."

The Art of Guilt
Guilt is one of the suffering parent's favorite gifts.

After I got married and left home every Christmas I would to go back to Tennessee to visit, because our mama said she just couldn't have a Christmas if her babies didn't all come back home. After three years David and I moved out to Phoenix, and of course I kept going home to Flat Rock every Christmas.

Finally, after more than a decade of traveling every December back to Tennessee, where it was cold, rainy, and dreary, I called home and said, "Mama, I'm so sorry, but we're not going to make it this Christmas. It costs us over $1,800 to fly home, and the weather here is so pretty, and so many of our friends here have open houses and parties every year, and we've never had the chance to attend them before, and we thought it would be nice to be with our friends, just this once. And we were just out there for Thanksgiving. So we've decided just to stay home in Phoenix this Christmas."

There was a dead silence on the phone. Finally Mama spoke up. She said, "Well, that's all right ... if you're not coming home, I won't bother fixing my fruitcakes and my jam cakes, and I won't bother getting a country ham. I always got one because you liked them so much, but I guess we won't be needing one this year.

"But you know," she continued on, "when you were just a little girl I used to have to wash out your clothes on an old washboard, and there were times my knuckles would bleed from washing out your clothes on that old washboard. And there were times when I needed new shoes, but I noticed my babies needed new shoes, and y'all always came first, and I remember how you always loved having a tree, but I guess we won't put up a tree this year ... anyway, y'all have a good Christmas."

That year I went home a week early.

It goes both ways: kids know how to put guilt on their parents, too, so I've experienced it coming from both directions.

In our home, Friday night was always Mexican food night. I absolutely love Mexican food, but my two boys were not big fans. (Which has made me wonder on occasion if they are really mine.)

One Friday afternoon I yelled outside for them, "Come on in and get cleaned up. Daddy'll be home soon. It's Friday night, and we're goin' out for Mexican food!"

A few minutes later they come dragging into the house, and Michael says, "Mama, we're not really going out for Mexican food *again* tonight, are we?"

"Yes, we are," I say, "It's Friday night, and I *deserve* Mexican food. I work hard for this family." (Being dramatic here.) "I cook, I clean, I wash clothes, I help with homework, and besides that, I go all over the world speaking to help us live. I have to go speak in places like Hilton Head, and Pinehurst, and Maui—I mean, I really *suffer* for this family."

Michael says, "But Mama, I was just next door telling Robby about your cornbread. I told him, 'Robby, you wouldn't believe it; even before I get in the house I can *smell* it cooking. My mama is the best cook in the world. I'll go stand in front of the stove and watch it turn all golden brown, and sometimes Mama will break off a hunk of that cornbread before supper's ready and slap some butter on it, and the steam comes up, and man! It's just delicious.'

"Mama," he continues, "you're not gonna believe this, but Robby has never in all his life had homemade cornbread! Mama, that is child abuse. I feel so sorry for him. He doesn't have the mama I have, that can make such delicious cornbread. Mama, I told him after dinner tonight, I was going to bring him a piece of cornbread. In fact, I think he's sitting right there on his front porch right now, expecting that cornbread and just thinking about how good it's gonna taste."

And then he looks up me, all innocent big eyes, and delivers the kill shot.

"Now, what am I going to tell him if we go out for Mexican food, and you don't make cornbread?"

Ten minutes later my husband walks into the kitchen, takes one look at me and says, "Rita, what are you doing?"

"What does it look like I'm doin'?" I snap. "I'm makin' cornbread!"

"But it's Friday night," he says. "How come you're making cornbread on Friday night?"

"I have no idea!"

As a parent, it's impossible to be perfect and easy to feel inadequate. But I've tried hard not to put too much guilt on myself. As Erma says, we do the best we can with what we have to work with.

When my boys were growing up, I actually was a perfect housekeeper. You probably think I'm joking, but it's the truth: you could even eat off of my floors. Really, you could. There was ketchup, mashed potatoes, and pork and beans all rubbed in there. I'm kidding, of course—but my point is, I decided early on that I'd rather spend more time with my family than to be the most meticulous housekeeper.

And homemade cookies? Oh, did I ever deliver homemade cookies. I remember slapping those Oreos in the oven, figuring they'd never know the difference. In fact, I could picture them someday, my boys all grown up and telling their wives, "My mama used to make us these homemade Oreos—it was so amazing, how she would get them all squishy and warm, right out of the oven."

Okay, so maybe I didn't bake as many cookies or scrub the kitchen floors as often as I'd have liked. But you know, I think my boys are going to remember more the times I spent with them, just talking to them, asking them what they'd dreamed about the night before, what they thought about, what they wanted to do with their lives. Those of us with children need to remind ourselves often: they are born *through* us, not necessarily *to* us. As Jackie Kennedy Onassis said, "If you bungle raising your children, I don't think anything else you do matters very much." And I'd do it all over again in a heartbeat. In all my life, I don't know that I've ever experienced anything more rewarding than knowing I've been there for my boys.

You can only count on having your children at home with you for eighteen summers. Make the most of your time together.

I was in Dallas to give a speech one night, and before leaving for the auditorium I called home to check on everything. When Scott got on the phone he said, "Mama, one of my goldfish died today."

"Oh, Honey, I'm so sorry," I said. "We'll bury it when I get home."

"It's all right, Mama," he said, "I already did. I buried it in a Cracker Jack box—with a little bit of water, just in case."

"Well," I thought, "I can't swear he got it from me, but my Lord has that boy learned something about optimism and the power of expectations."

Laugh at Any Age

Two things happened when I turned forty. First, God played a terrible trick on me. I woke up one morning and found that he had rearranged my whole body. Everything was suddenly three inches lower than where it belongs. And the second thing that happened… well, I forget what the second thing was.

Oh wait. That's right. The second thing was that my memory started going. You know why God doesn't want you to have kids after you're forty? Because you'd forget where you left them.

If you got this far in life thinking humor wasn't all that important, wait till you start noticing that you're aging. Things will start getting funny pretty fast. At least you hope they do. As Daddy always said, life is like a roll of toilet paper: the closer you get to the end, the faster it goes.

After a lifetime of hard work, my daddy retired at the age of seventy-six, at which point he took his first airplane flight ever when he flew to Phoenix to visit us. (The skycap could tell Daddy was *country* when he asked, "Is this your bag, sir?" and Daddy replied, "Naw, it's my brother-in-law's, but he said I could borrow it.") As soon as he'd rested up, I drove Daddy the couple hundred miles north to go see the Grand Canyon. I was telling him all about it, bragging on it so much you'd have thought I had something to do with creating it, I so wanted him to be impressed. "Daddy," I said, "do you know it took millions of years to develop this place?"

"Huh," he said. "Was it a government job?"

We took him to have his eyes examined so he could renew his driver's license. The young doctor said, "Sir, how far can you see at your age?"

He said, "Son, I can see pretty far."

"I'm sorry," the doctor pressed, "but that's not what I meant. I need to know, *how* far can you see?"

And Daddy said, "Well, Son, I can see the moon. How far is that?"

Because he had just retired from being a mechanic, I had new business cards printed up for him. Underneath his name, it said retired. In the upper right-hand corner it said, no phone, and in the upper left-hand corner, no address. In the lower left-hand corner, no money, and the lower right-hand corner, no worries. That Sunday he went all through the crowd at church, passing out his business card. You'd have thought he was J. Paul Getty. It's amazing what it did for his self-esteem.

Perspective and Sanity

One of the greatest causes of stress in our lives is change, and on that score, I've got some bad news, and some good news.

First, the bad news: As much change as you've already seen in your life, you're going to see more. Change is going to keep happening, whether you want it to or not.

Now, are you ready for the good news? Here it is: As much change as you've already seen in your life, you're going to see more. Change is going to keep happening, whether you want it to or not.

Change is the one constant. Pretty much everything you've got going on in your life is going to change, and you might as well get in touch with it, and get over it, right now. You can either decide to adjust or become a very unhappy person.

The thing that's tricky about this is that we are biologically programmed to *resist* change. We'll do anything we can to keep our body temperature at 98.6° and our pH at 7.35. On the level of biology, that's a good thing, but played out on the stage of your major life events, it doesn't work the same way. Resisting change produces a life of stress, tension, pain, and disappointment. Instead, we can train ourselves to use change as an endless source of inspiration, motivation, creativity, and productivity. It means embracing change instead of resisting it.

And frankly, I don't think it's possible to do that without a whopping big sense of humor.

On the very first page of this book, I pointed out that humor helps keep things in perspective—and even when it doesn't succeed in doing that, at least it keeps us sane. As the 1980s grew up and started aiming toward the 1990s, the need for perspective and sanity in my life grew right along with it.

Cookbooks and Infomercials

Despite the show's growing popularity it still wasn't paying all that much, and even though I was starting to earn some money as a speaker, the television schedule imposed pretty severe limits on how many speeches I could fly around and deliver. With our young family and our extended family's growing economic needs, there came a point when I knew I had to find some way to bring more money in the door. So I did what we call a *personal inventory*: what skills, talents, passions, and resources did I have? In the *passions* department, I put down, "loves to cook." Okay ... but how was that going to ever make me money? I sure wasn't about to start a restaurant.

And then, once again, I thought of Miss Daisy and her success with the cookbook I'd suggested she write. Hey, why not? I could write a cookbook too.

If one was good, two must be better. In 1976, I wrote *De Grazia & Mexican Cookery* illustrated by the famous southwestern artist Ted De Grazia, who had been a guest on my show and had become a close friend, and the following year I published my own *Sourdough Cookery*.

It's funny how things turn out. When David and I first moved to Phoenix I'd been pursuing my master's degree, but once I started working at Channel 5 I knew I was never going to pursue teaching as a career and didn't really need that education degree. So while I did complete all my course work, I never finished my thesis. Until now, that was. As far as I was concerned, the cookbooks *were* my master's thesis. And as theses go, they did pretty well: the two books together sold more than a million and a half copies.

A few years later, I wrote another book, mainly so I'd have something I could refer to in my talks. *Making Time, Making Money*, published by St. Martin's Press in 1982, was basically a book on how to manage a busy life and stay sane. They say we teach best that which we most need to learn. Case in point: This was something I was now teaching around the country in my speaking engagements and at the same time something I was also learning by the seat of my pants. Between crisscrossing the country giving speeches, promoting the books, taping the show five days a week, and managing a growing family, things were getting fairly crazy. And then they got crazier.

A few years later, I got involved in creating several infomercials.

We produced the first infomercial in 1987, thanks to the generosity and genius of Ray Lindstrom of Media Arts, promoting a set of motivational cassette tapes titled *It's Time for You.* My friend Dr. Shad Helmstetter suggested the title, since the cassette program was based on roughly the same ideas as in my St. Martin's book. Two years later, with the help of my friends Pam Daily and Mark Fornier, we produced a second infomercial. This one was a little different and reflected the amount of public speaking I had done in the two years in between. This one was called *Laugh Your Way to Success.*

Because there were still so few infomercials on television (comparatively speaking), I soon became kind of a nationally known figure and started being bombarded with speaking requests.

But wait—as they used to say in certain late-night infomercials (though I never did say it in mine)—*there's more!*

Then it got even crazier.

A Skinny White Oprah?

By the late 1980s my television show had become enormously popular. Our demographics were off the charts and our show was constantly sold out. Our ratings at the time were much higher than anything even Oprah would enjoy twenty years later, because in those days people didn't have a hundred cable stations to choose from and were still largely watching their three network channels and whatever local independent channels might be available.

One day in 1987 my boss got a call from Earl Greenburg, who was vice president of daytime programming for NBC. Earl had happened to catch one of my infomercials late one night. He got curious about me and did a little digging, managed to catch a few of my shows, and decided that I should be the next national talk show host—a skinny white Southern Oprah. (Oprah's show had just gone national a few years earlier and was rapidly gaining popularity.)

"Look," said Earl, "I want to talk to you about doing a syndicated show with Rita Davenport. I think she should be in homes coast to coast."

He lined everything up and got the same syndicators who were distributing Sally Jesse Raphael's show to work on it. For the next six months we poured hundreds of hours and the Gaylord Production Company poured about three-quarters of a million dollars into the project, traveling all over the country to shoot half a dozen pilot segments. It was dizzying, exciting, and exhausting. And the whole while, I found myself feeling increasingly ambivalent about what we were doing.

On the one hand, it was an absolutely enormous, mind-boggling opportunity. While the trend in daytime talk shows was moving toward a more sensational, tabloid-style, scandal-laced format based on titillation and outrageousness, my show would emphasize the inspirational and motivational, along with a gentler sort of humor. If we succeeded, the new show had the potential to make me a household name from coast to coast. Talk about touching lives and making a difference!

At the same time, I was not as excited about doing this show as I'd expected to be. The truth was, I had never been that motivated to take my television career beyond our local audience. I didn't especially want to leave Phoenix and move to New York City or Los Angeles, where the national action was happening. I'd had offers to do that in the past, but I was very happy where we were, raising our kids in Phoenix. I was happy in local television. I wasn't making much money at it, but between the books, infomercials, and speeches, I was making a pretty good income on the side, and David's job as an engineering manager still provided our major source of income.

I also was not that thrilled with the format of the show. For one thing, it was all scripted, with cue cards and everything. When I did my local show, I had my guests lined up and knew generally what I would be doing, but it was more extemporaneous. I didn't have any scripts or cue cards, and used the TelePrompTer only for introductions. But for a nationally syndicated show, they wanted to exercise a tighter level of control over the content, and even hired a team of writers.

In some ways producing those pilot episodes was a nightmare. One day on the set our cue card guy, John, was not turning the cue cards quite fast enough, and I was getting to the end of each card before the next one was ready, which meant the pacing was a little awkward and jerky. Our assistant producer fired him on the spot.

He just about broke down right there in front of all of us. "Please" he said, "I've got to have this job!"

I happened to know that John had five kids to feed, and I butted in, saying to the assistant producer, "It's okay, I can slow down a little."

But she wouldn't budge. John had to pack his stuff and leave the set right then and there.

I was heartbroken. That night in my suite at the Beverly Hills Wilshire Hotel, I got down on my knees and said, "God, this just doesn't feel right. If this is what you want me to do, I'll do it, because I'm here to fulfill whatever assignment you've got for me. But it sure doesn't feel right."

It *wasn't* right.

After six months and dozens of negotiated deals with channel affiliates around the country, we came within four markets of making the quota that would have made the syndication deal work—just inches short of the finish line.

The Other Side of Failure

Soon after the syndication deal collapsed, I had lunch with Erma Bombeck and explained the whole thing to her, what a great opportunity it would have been and how close we came to making it happen, how much time and money and effort we'd spent on it, and what a failure it had turned out to be.

"Why do you say that?" she asked.

"Well, Erma," I said, "you wouldn't know what failure

is, and if you ever did know you've probably forgotten it by now."

"Really," she replied drily.

"Well, sure," I said. "I mean, look at you. You're so successful it's not funny!" (Which come to think of it, considering the nature of her particular career, was a pretty ironic way of putting it.)

"Ah," she said, and she looked at me. "Rita, can I ask you something?" I nodded and said, of course she could. "You know anybody who wants any 1985 calendars?"

I was puzzled. "No. Why would anybody want a 1985 calendar in 1988?"

She said, "Apparently they wouldn't. And I'm sitting on 200,000 of 'em that didn't sell when we first offered them. If you know anyone who's got a serious case of 1985 nostalgia and would like to buy our entire inventory, let me know."

I had nothing to say to that.

Then she said, "You remember that program I produced a few years ago? The syndicated show?" I remembered it, all right: it was a sitcom called *Maggie* that ran eight episodes, got terrible reviews, and made poor Erma incredibly overworked in the process, until it was mercifully canceled.

"Oh," I said. "Right. Good point."

"I'll tell you the truth," she said. "I'm so glad that show didn't work out. One full season of that, and I would have been worn to a shred."

I had to admit, she was right ... and the same thing was true for me. I knew that in the long run, I would be grateful that the syndication never went through.

This was a turning point in my life. It *looked* like I had failed, but there was a whole other side to it that I had not been giving its due. I had learned a great deal, and it was feedback that would help me change my direction. In fact, it would help push me onto the course my life would take for the decades that followed.

Failure is simply the negative feedback that gives us the opportunity to practice; its purpose is to show us that the path we were trying out wasn't the ideal one for us. There's nothing wrong with failing—unless you use it as an excuse to shy away from developing your gifts and pursuing your purpose in life. When some effort of yours fails, you can let it shut you down, in which case you withdraw into yourself, get bitter, and shrink from making other new efforts. Or you can use it as an opportunity to learn, grow, and get fired up. You're going to make some wrong decisions in your life. And you've got to have some valleys in your life, so you can appreciate the peak experiences. But you can't give up on yourself. If you don't believe in yourself, nobody else will believe in you either, and that makes doing anything practically impossible.

Failure is also one more opportunity to develop a strong sense of humor. Have you ever had something happen that seemed just awful at the time, yet months or years later you found yourself laughing about it? Here's what you do. First, get into the habit of saying, "Someday we're going to laugh about this." And after you've said that, then say, "Hey, why wait?"

The secret is to laugh sooner.

I was speaking in front of 700 people in Houston one night, and as I walked onstage I happened to look down— and noticed I had a string of toilet paper about two feet long caught on the heel of my shoe, trailing along behind me. Option A: turn tail and run backstage. Option B: start to cry. I went with Option C: I started laughing. I survived the night just fine. Hey, I was grateful it wasn't in my panty hose. You're going to have disasters large and small happen to you. It's just the way it is. You've got to be able to laugh.

A Valuable Four-Letter Word

When the syndication project came to a halt, the whole experience brought a number of four-letter words to mind. (Don't forget, I'd learned a lot about language from being driven to school by my daddy.) In the end, though, I summed up the episode with a different four-letter word, once I'd been reminded of it by my eight-year-old son Scott.

Scott was in third grade at the time and had a skating

party coming up. I picked him up from school that day, and as he climbed into the car he said, "Mama, I asked Nicole to skate with me."

Nicole—right, that was the little girl he really liked. He'd talked about her before. My heart started beating and I thought, "Oh my goodness, what if she said no? What if he got rejected? I just wonder what that little third-grade hussy said to him."

You know how mamas are about their little boys.

"Scott," I said, "what did she say?" Then I held my breath.

"She said yes, Mama."

I let out my breath. Thank you Lord, I thought. I'll bet that little girl is just the sweetest, smartest little thing. She's got a good head on her, that one. Obviously, my son has excellent taste in women.

But then I started thinking, sure, this went well today, but what about the future? I need to make sure my son is prepared for disappointment. Because someday, some little girl's going to say no when he asks her to skate or to a dance or out on a date.

"Scott," I said, "how would you have felt if Nicole had said no?"

He said, "Oh, Mama, there's seventeen other girls in my class! I'd just ask the next girl."

I thought about Erma and her calendars and her failed sitcom, and about our syndicated national television show that was never going to happen, and I thought, *My son has got it exactly right.* That was the four-letter word I needed.

Next!

It occurred to me that maybe this was just like our house being struck by lightning. There was God's sense of humor again. He took me just *this* close to putting me on a national platform where I would be broadcasting into homes all across America ... and then went, "Nahh, I was just kidding. I've got something completely different in mind for you."

And boy, did he ever.

Chapter 9

WHO'S GOT YOUR BACK?

My brother, Ray, missed the first grade of school because as a child he had nephritis, which is inflammation of the kidneys. Doctor Weaver recommended months of bed rest. As a result, since Ray was somewhat small for his age, he was never really encouraged to participate in sports, and certainly not expected to excel. He played left field in Knothole League baseball, never missed a practice—and sat on the bench for the whole four years. Finally, in the last game, the coach let him play one inning since his team was so far ahead. He was so excited; at least he made it onto the field during a game!

In high school he tried out for the Glencliff High School track team. He didn't make the team, but helped out as a waterboy for his freshman and most of his sophomore years. Toward the end of his sophomore year, he participated in a district track meet as a helper—sitting on the bench, as usual. The team was doing pretty well and had won a couple of events when the coaches discovered their numbers were down, and they were in danger of being disqualified. At that point, a student teacher named Phillip Saindon, who was a friend of mine, spotted Ray and ran over to explain the situation. He asked Ray if he could suit up and just make it around the track, didn't matter what speed, just so they wouldn't be disqualified from the meet. They found him some gym shorts, though they were so big he literally had to hold them up to keep them from falling off (he weighed only 116 pounds) and a pair of size 8 track shoes he could use (though he wore a size 6).

Ray was entered in the 440 meter event. He was so unaccustomed to competing that he was startled when the starting gun was fired. Ray had never been coached in how to pace himself, starting at a moderate speed and then speeding up halfway through the race, so he ran at his top speed the entire race—and won with a record-breaking time!

The coaches stared at each other in shock, realizing that this kid who'd sat on the bench for all these years was in fact a very talented runner. They put him in two other events that day and he won all three while holding up his shorts and wearing shoes that were two sizes too big.

When I picked him up, I noticed him limping to the car. I jumped out, panicked, afraid he'd been hurt, and asked what had happened. He told me that running in those ill-fitting shoes had given him terrible blood blisters on his feet. And then he told me how well he had run when he had gotten his big break.

From then on Phillip and the coach worked with Ray. I am still so grateful to my friend for giving my little brother the break of a lifetime. The local press nicknamed him "Rabbit," because he was so small and so fast. He went on to break records in numerous track events and was even named Athlete of the Year for all of Tennessee, receiving a huge plaque and a full-page photo in the newspaper.

Ray always said, "Never look back when you're running, because it only causes you to lose momentum." I've found that a pretty good lesson in general.

Once, when he won a state championship event and broke his own record in the 440 meter, I asked why he'd run faster that day.

"Did you train more, get more rest, or eat better?" I asked. "What was it that caused you to run faster?"

"I just had to," he replied. "Those were the fastest kids in the whole state. If I was going to win, I just had to stay ahead of them. I paced myself to be faster and stay ahead— no matter what!" That's turned out to be a pretty good life lesson, too.

After graduating from high school, Ray went on to get a full-ride athletic scholarship at MTSU—still weighing just 116 pounds and wearing size 6 shoes.

Dr. Weaver once got the chance to see Ray race. He couldn't believe that his patient, that sickly little boy whose life he'd probably saved when he was in the first grade, was the same kid who was out there now, tearing around that track with a whole crowd cheering him on.

Ray went on to be a sergeant on the Nashville police force. I'm sure there wasn't a single criminal who ever succeeded in outrunning the law when my brother was the one in pursuit.

I believe one of the reasons each one of us is here is to be a witness to others, and to help them discover the greatness that lies inside them. If it hadn't been for Phillip and that coach, Ray would've likely never known he was a talented runner.

What Rays are in *your* life, waiting for you to give them their big break and discover the incredible runner living inside of them?

Who's Got Your Back?

In the middle of 1990 my daddy died, and six months later we lost my little brother Ray to lymphoma after a failed bone marrow transplant. Ray desperately wanted to live, but it was not to be. He was just forty-five years old.

In the course of less than a year, our family had suddenly gotten a whole lot smaller.

Ray was a cop in Nashville, and no one knows the value of a team like a city cop. To a lot of us, "I've got your back" is a phrase; to Ray and his buddies, it was an everyday life-

or-death truth. For that matter, it's really a life-or-death truth to you and me, too, even if your business doesn't happen to be one that puts you in the path of desperate people with Glocks shoved into their waistbands. No matter what you do in your life and work, your success ultimately depends on who you have around you—on who's got your back.

Reading my story, you may have gotten the impression that I was pretty sure of myself from a young age. But the truth is, I was very shy as a child, and it took me a long time to develop the level of confidence that allowed me to do some of the things I've done. The only way I could have ever developed that kind of confidence was by gathering around me a support team of friends who would give me good counsel, forgive my worst shortcomings, and believe in me, often more than I did myself.

We need people around us who make us feel good about ourselves. Isn't that why we have dogs? When you get home at night, your dog is always happy to see you and tell you how wonderful you are. Once when David and I had recently gotten a new dog, I told him, "You know, I think you love this dog more than you do me." And he said, "Well, if you greeted me every day wagging your tail and licking my face, I might love you that much too!"

I saw a wonderful bumper sticker once; it said, "I wish I were half the person my dog thinks I am." The people on my support team over the years have been a lot like the dog on the bumper sticker.

"Old friends are gold," goes the saying, "new friends are silver." This is so true, and if you have at least five good friends when you come to the end of your life, you are truly blessed. I realized this when my dear friend Sharon Overstake passed away and the hospital waiting room was filled with her friends. That outpouring of love made her one of the most blessed people I had ever known.

Time for a Change ... Again

One person who made our lives possible was David's mother, Sue, who was the only parent David had ever really known. David's father died in a freak accident at a munitions factory when David himself was not yet two years old, and in one of those awful runs of bad fortune that seem to be placed in our lives to try the mettle of our souls, David's older brother, who was barely five years old, died six months later from complications of an illness. Sue had been through a lot.

We called her Mama Sue, but when Michael started talking he called her Mama Too, and the name stuck. In fact, it was perfect for her—because she was indeed another mama to the boys. She told me that when I had a second child, she would come out to Phoenix to help us. That turned out to be an understatement. After Scott was born, she retired from work (she had built a beauty shop in her home to make ends meet) and moved to Phoenix, where she lived for the rest of her life. The boys never had a baby-sitter growing up: they had either me or Mama Too. She drove them to school, stayed around and did volunteer work there while they were in class, and was there for them when they got out. She was more than a grandmother; she was my right hand and sometimes my left hand, too, and raised those boys right along with their Mama One. Mama Too was such a gift in our lives. She was with us until 2010, when she passed away at the age of ninety-five and a half.

Mama Too's help notwithstanding, by the time Daddy and Ray passed away in 1990, things in my life had gotten awfully hectic.

When the syndicated show didn't make it, I had continued building my speaking career, selling books and tapes through my infomercials, and doing my cooking show in Phoenix that aired five days a week. By 1989 it was clear that I had too much on my plate. Something had to give. It was time to leave the show. I went to my boss, Dick DeAngelis, who was Channel 5's general manager, and said, "I'm so sorry, but I just can't keep doing this."

He was incredibly understanding and had always been very supportive of my speaking endeavors. He wished me the very best and agreed to cancel my show. Talk about someone having your back. I'll always be grateful for Dick DeAngelis, program director Chuck Alvey, and my talented crew.

So I left Channel 5 to become a full-time speaker, and that year, the hillbilly kid with the speech defect did 118 speeches, or roughly one every three days. I was racking up more frequent flier miles than some airline pilots. But the cosmic joke wasn't over—the wheel of career change hadn't finished with me yet.

Direct Selling?!

For years, my brother Ray had urged me to get involved in direct selling, to do a business like Amway, Herbalife, or Mary Kay. Sometimes he would get into one himself, just dabbling, really, but dabbling in earnest, and he'd say, "Gayle, you need to get into this. You'd be great at it." And every time he did, I thought, "Heck, I'm a television personality. I'm a speaker. I don't have time to do something like that"—like I was above it all or something.

I admit I let my ego cloud my judgment at first. But then I flashed on feedback I'd gotten once from my friend Bob Haley when he heard me speak at the Opryland Hotel in Nashville. First he gave me his sincere congratulations, which I appreciated—and then he said something that really hit me. "Rita, you do a great job, and I know you're really successful as a speaker ... but what would you do if you lost your voice?" Yikes. I hadn't thought about that. What was my plan B? As far as my income was concerned, did I even *have* a plan B?

As I said, Ray really understood the importance of building a team. He knew that you can't make it in life on your own. As I was soon to learn, that is especially true in the world of direct selling. What matters in direct selling, ultimately, is not what *you* can do or what *you* can accomplish as much as whom you can attract to your team and how well you can support and encourage them to become their best. Because they, and the people they bring, and the people *they* bring, will together accomplish far more than you could ever dream of achieving on your own. Every whale knows a minnow and every minnow knows a whale.

I knew a little bit about direct selling, network marketing, multilevel, MLM, party plan—by whatever name, I got the general idea. A company with a unique, truly great product line would decide that, rather than sell their products through a more conventional chain of wholesaler and retailers, shops, and store shelves, they would instead sell them through a homegrown network of independent representatives, typically spearheaded by some of the product's most enthusiastic users. It was an idea that had been around since the fifties, best known through a few household-name companies such as Amway, Avon, and Mary Kay. (I had even interviewed Mary Kay a few times and had the honor of sharing the platform with her in the late eighties.)

I'd known of such companies, although not in any detail or that up close and personal, and knew how the business principle worked. In fact, I'd given speeches at quite a few conventions for direct selling companies before, including Amway, Jafra, Mary Kay, Pampered Chef, Tupperware, and others.

Back in 1987, a good two years before I left the television show, Laura Fletcher, an independent consultant for a little cosmetics-and-personal-care company, heard me speak and thought I would be a good speaker to hire for one of their business conventions. She got in touch with Petter Morck, the company's founder, and urged him to have me speak at their next event.

Petter called me up on the phone. It was quite a conversation: a native of Norway, Petter could barely speak English, and at the same time, I'm sure he must have thought that whatever it was I was talking, it wasn't any kind of English he'd ever heard. Somehow we managed to communicate, though, and he invited me to speak at an event they would be holding in Vail, Colorado.

The company was still tiny at this point, and there were fewer than a hundred people at that event. But Petter got so much feedback from the talk and felt that I'd had such an impact on the results his people started getting afterward that he invited me to speak again six months later, this time in New York City.

There are thousands of companies in the world of direct selling. I knew enough about the business to know that which company you join is a huge key to your success. It's far from the only key, because ultimately *you* are the one who determines your success, and the particular team of independent representatives you choose to work with also plays a big role. But if you want to achieve any level of real success, you need to align yourself with a company that really knows what it's doing—and that means choosing a company that realizes direct sales/network marketing is a personal development business, disguised as a business selling selected products. Make sure they know it's a heart to heart, people business and has a charitable spirit.

Despite Ray's urging, I had never seriously considered joining one of these fine companies before—but something clicked for me now. It was time for me to get into direct selling/network marketing. I was captivated by the idea this business was a level playing field for all. I fell in love with the people involved, and realized that the most exciting dynamic was the social interaction. Donna Johnson (who sponsored my sister, and consequently me too), Thea O'Donoghue, Phoebe Fournier, Jacque Carlson, and others welcomed us with love, support, and encouragement. Some even flew to Phoenix to help me with needed training. And I was quite frankly blown away by the opportunity. I thought network marketing using direct sales had enormous potential. I still was not that interested in the idea of building a business myself, but I thought it would be a great way to help support my sister. *Okay,* I thought, *I'm going to get into this for Euphiazene.*

Euphiazene
Nothing happens in life without the help of others. Van Gogh was one of the world's greatest painters—but his personal

life was a mess. If it hadn't been for his pub-owner brother Theo, who supported him and kept him fed and clothed, we wouldn't have his art today.

Now neither of us paint and (thank heavens) neither of our personal lives is a mess, and what's more, nobody in my family has ever owned a pub. So don't read more into the Van Gogh illustration than there is, but a huge part of my life in direct selling was motivated by a desire to help my sister and her now-disabled husband, Lucion. With my encouragement, Euphiazene joined first, then sponsored me, and we went up the ranks and built a large business together. Before getting into direct selling, she had been laid off from her job in a wave of downsizing. Years later she would often say, "How grateful I am for that pink slip!"

Our lives and careers after we each left home and before we became involved in direct selling could not have been more different, and yet here we were, our professional lives suddenly intertwined. Ray was both amazed and thrilled. One of my greatest regrets is that, although Ray had encouraged us on this course, his battle with cancer prevented him from being a part of our team, and he did not live to see our sister's success, and years later, his own daughter, Stephanie Anderson, and son, Jason McWhorter, grow *their* network marketing/direct selling businesses. We all felt we were building a business on his behalf, and that he would have loved being a part of the profession along with us.

A big part of creating success in direct selling is determined by how much energy and focus you put into reaching out and helping others. Nobody understands this better than Euphiazene—and she is one of the most generous people I know. She has had so much to overcome in her life, and she has overcome it all—and done it always with so much grace and good humor. Everyone who knows her loves her; when she walks onto the stage for an event, the applause is thunderous, simply because of who she is. She also happens to be one of the best cooks in the world. We had dinner at her house just the other day, and my now-grown son Michael said, "Well, I believe this is the best meal I've ever had in my life." I said, "Well, thanks a lot—your mother hosted a cooking show and wrote two cookbooks!" He was right, though.

Euphiazene and I both did well with our businesses. We joined our company in 1987, and within less than a year I became a Regional Vice President, which at the time was the topmost achievement level in the company. Within the year I went on to win the Parade of Champions, based on my sales and sponsoring numbers, and the annual President's Award, given for the highest growth percentage in the company.

In 1990 Petter and I starting talking about the possibility of my becoming more directly involved in the company's future. The following year, at a national Management Training Seminar in California, he made an announcement: the company had a new president.

No wonder that syndication deal had never gone through. Clearly, I had a very different assignment to carry out.

In the President's Chair

I still had a handful of speaking commitments and I continued to do a few talks here and there, just to keep my name out there and maintain my sense of timing. (Gotta keep up the skills, you know.) But for all practical purposes, I now had a new career, and it was one I would continue for the next twenty years.

Being a company president was a daunting and complicated task. I think the only reason I was able to pull it off was due to my experience at the television station. It certainly wasn't my formal business training. (I didn't have any.) But all those years producing my own television show had to some extent groomed me for this challenge. As the show's producer, I was considered a manager at Channel 5, with a staff and budget challenges, and went to all the management meetings. It was a small operation, but it was my training ground and I paid attention. And I'd read and interviewed enough Peter Druckers, Jack Welches, Tom Peterses, Stephen Coveys, and all the other great business management writers to give me a solid sense of the fundamental elements of what makes a good leader.

Basically these lessons boiled down to two: 1) surround yourself with the right people, and 2) treat them well by providing that morale-producing environment.

From the start I was deeply engaged in the nuts and bolts of running the company. As soon as I could, I brought in Greg Lechowski, a Notre Dame graduate, to serve as our CFO and started building a strong executive team. During those first few years I was extremely hands-on in an operational way, but as we got the right people in place at headquarters, bit by bit I started being able to become more engaged in the field, motivating, training, and inspiring the people who were on the front lines.

Soon it became clear that this was truly what I did best. One day our CEO, Steve Biroczky, said to me, "Rita, every day you spend in this office is a waste of a day! You need to be out inspiring people and raising the bar of their expectations, teaching and training them in the nuts and bolts of how to do their business and how to stay inspired enough to do it long enough to achieve success for themselves. You've walked the walk—and they need to hear how you did it so they can do it, too."

As we continued to grow I spent more and more time in the field, being on the road as much as twenty days a month and sometimes even more. Over the years I racked up three million miles on American Airlines alone.

On a Mission

Earlier I talked about the importance of getting completely comfortable with being yourself. One of the beauties of feeling good about being yourself is that it puts you in a place where you're happy to let everyone else be *themselves*, too. You may be smarter than I am, or younger than I am, or more hip than I am. You may live in a bigger house, or have that great singing voice that I'd always wished I'd had. But whatever you have, I'm not jealous of you. Why would I be? Your being the best *you* possible doesn't take anything away from me being the best *me* possible. I love having friends around me who are much more accomplished than I am. I *want* you to do your best. I'm going to be applauding you and cheering you across the finish line, no matter what. Every true mentor wants their mentee to outdo them.

And that's the core of what became my career for the next twenty years.

I had a big vision for our company, and I took that vision very seriously. That vision was all about what this business could mean to the individual consultant—which in many cases would be a woman who had never carved out a career with their own business before.

I could see that if you put in the sweat equity, no matter how little you started with or how impoverished you were, you could become very successful in this business, and you could do so *without* having to scare up the capital it would take to invest, say, in a McDonald's or a Subway, and you could do so *without* having to go get an MBA or Ph.D. first. Direct selling provides a level playing field, offering everyone the same opportunity regardless of race, gender, religion, or education. I knew that if I had known about an opportunity like this when I was living in Flat Rock, Tennessee, I would have poured my whole self into it and done really well. (Matter of fact, I *did* pour my whole self into it and do really well.)

This became a consuming passion for me. Yes, it was a job, but it became more; it became a personal mission. It seemed to me that direct selling could solve needs that our social welfare system was supposed to solve but didn't always do such a great job of solving. And direct selling could do that for tens and hundreds of thousands of people. When you come right down to it, this was really just one more chapter added on to my days as a social worker.

I became absorbed in a mission to make people aware of this profession and what they could be, do, and have with a direct selling business opportunity. I coached each representative I worked with to be the person she wanted to be—and that if they would do what it takes, they would have what they dreamed of having. The best thing I could do was to serve them, in person, up close and personal, hands-on, day in and day out. I ate it, slept it, and drank it with passion and constancy, twenty-four hours a day and seven days a week. That's what it takes, needs, and deserves. You can also build slowly at your own pace to accommodate your family's needs.

In 1995 I opened up our home for a special promotion incentive challenge: people who hit certain benchmarks would be flown in to come visit us. We called this program "Areas in Paradise." ("Area" was a specific achievement title people needed to hit to qualify for this adventure, and the little town outside Phoenix where we live is called Paradise Valley.) I wanted them to be able to walk through our home I was so proud of (yes, this is the one that within a year would be struck by lightning!) and say, "She grew up in a house that didn't even have a bathroom, and look, she's got six bathrooms now." I wanted them to come and see for themselves what this opportunity could do for them, too!

During my time with Channel 5 I had created a collage on one wall in our home with pictures of movie stars, rocks stars, presidents and senators, moguls and millionaires I had interviewed. Some of the people whose signed pictures ended up in that collage included:

> Muhammad Ali, Eddie Arnold, Jack Benny, Milton Berle, Amanda Blake (Miss Kitty from *Gunsmoke*), Vida Blue, Erma Bombeck, Jeff Bridges, Les Brown, President George H. W. Bush, Vincent Bugliosi (author of *Helter Skelter*), Glen Campbell, Roy Clark, Bill Cosby, Jamie Lee Curtis, Hugh Downs, Wayne Dyer, Dick Van Dyke, James Garner, Alex Haley (author of *Roots*), Mark Harmon, Mark Victor Hansen, Florence Henderson, William Holden, Diane Ladd, Jay Leno, Sugar Ray Leonard, Jerry Lewis, Harvey Mackay, Bill Murray, Jim Nabors, Governor Janet Napolitano, Marie Osmond,

Dolly Parton, Robert Redford, Oscar de la
Renta, Burt Reynolds, Don Rickles, Joan Rivers,
Roy Rogers, Richard Simmons, Frank Sinatra Jr.,
Red Skelton, Roger Staubach, Gloria Steinem,
Hervé Jean-Pierre Villechaize (who played
Tattoo the dwarf on *Fantasy Island*), John Wayne,
and Zig Ziglar.

Now I started adding onto that collage new photos of
the leaders in our organization. People would come visit
my house and see their own face looking back at them, right
next to Jeff Bridges, Jamie Lee Curtis, Robert Redford, and
John Wayne. As I later learned, they would go through my
entire house—cabinets, closets, drawers, everything. I had
monogrammed toilet paper with D's, and people would
tear off a square and take it home with them for framing, as
if they were at Graceland or Dollywood. It was an absolute
blast! They would all get into my bathtub and have their
picture taken. These women would just go nuts, they were
so excited—and what they were excited about really had
nothing to do with me or our home. It was about being
acknowledged for what they had achieved so far, and about
the enormous possibilities of what they could go on to
achieve.

I had made our home into a living, breathing message:

*I did this, and you can do this too. This is something
you can create. If I can do it, you can do it.*

To me, this was way more important than sitting in a
boardroom or poring over financial projections day in and
day out. Don't get me wrong: those things had to be done,
and they had to be done right and to a T of competence,
which was exactly why I put such care into bringing together
the right executive team. But I saw clearly that for a direct
selling company, it's not the executive team at headquarters
who drives the growth of the company. The people in the
field do that. The corporate team is there to serve the field:

the people on the front lines, the "boots on the ground," the people building their business and their dreams one customer at a time. They are the ones who literally build the company. They truly are a company within a company, and they need to be acknowledged and appreciated, cheered and championed, at every opportunity. People will always work harder for praises than they will for raises.

I started sending people personal notes of encouragement and calling them on the phone. You never knew where these conversations would go. Sometimes I'd find myself saying, "Your husband's got questions about your new business? Put him on, let me talk to him!" Pretty soon I was making more than five hundred phone calls a month. I'd try three times, and if I didn't reach the person at that point I'd leave a message. I'd congratulate them, and tell them how proud of them I was and how much I appreciated them, and then sign off saying, "I'm gonna call ya'll back, now, when you get to the next level."

I knew how much this could mean from firsthand experience. Once, after I'd given a keynote speech for the National Speakers Association's annual national convention, I received a phone message from the famed CSP, CPAE Hall of Fame speaker Joel Weldon, who was just calling to encourage me and let me know he thought I'd done a terrific job. That message meant so much to me that I saved it, and anytime I felt insecure (and trust me, we all do from time to time!) I would revisit that message from Joel. I've listened to that message now for years.

And that's exactly what started happening with the messages I was leaving for our leaders. Some people, upon reaching an achievement title, would take their cellphones to bed with them at night just to make sure they didn't miss the congratulations call they were anticipating. Some saved these messages for years, playing them over and over and letting their teams hear them. When they would get discouraged they would play the message again, and it would empower them to keep going and persevere.

It wasn't that I said anything brilliant, or that there

was anything special about me in particular. It was that the company president was taking the time to place a personal phone call to them and tell them how much she appreciated them. Which I did! They were the people who were making this whole business work; they were the ones who were causing us to grow like spring mushrooms. Those of us at the home office weren't creating any of this growth, we were just there to keep up with them and do our best to support their efforts with products and incentive campaigns—*they* were the heroes of this story. And I wanted to make sure they knew that, and that they knew I *knew* that.

I wanted to make this company hugely successful—not for my own sake, but for all the powerfully positive impacts it would have on so many others if we did. I was already enjoying a financially blessed life before a career in network marketing. You can only eat at so many restaurants, drive so many cars, and have so many houses. (I mean, how many bathrooms can one family use?) But my dream was bigger than the biggest home David and I could possibly inhabit. My dream was this: *How many people can I help while I'm here on this earth?* If success is living your life the way you choose to live it, I wanted to help create a way that thousands of people could live that definition of success. *Where they could be more, do more, and have more, where they could learn more and earn more so they could share more.*

That was my motto, and in time it became a mantra of many others, too.

Explosion

In the sixties and seventies, the business community at large tended to look askance at direct selling. Somehow, in their eyes, it wasn't quite as "real" as more conventional forms of business. The eighties saw an explosion in the direct selling industry, with new companies springing up and doing fabulously well and some of the older companies showing continued strong growth as well—but it still was not accorded all that much more respect in the business world at large.

That all changed in the nineties. As the industry itself grew more sophisticated and professional, and as the leading companies continued to mature and grow, professionals from all walks of business started taking direct selling seriously. We started seeing doctors, lawyers, engineers, professors, and all sorts of prominent businesspeople staking their claim in this new territory. Worldwide, the direct selling industry grew to more than $100 billion in sales, and it finally began to attract serious attention from major investors, Wall Street, and the mainstream business and popular media.

This was the backdrop against which our company began to flourish and grow.

I'll never forget the day in 1992 that we first hit a million dollars in gross monthly sales. It was a watershed moment; we celebrated in the office with champagne and gave every employee a bonus. And we continued to grow, and grow some more.

Our company had first been launched in Switzerland in 1975 and started doing business in the United States in 1980. By the time I joined the company in 1987 it was still relatively tiny, with somewhat fewer than one thousand active consultants involved. By 2006, we were bringing in an average of 90,000 new people every *month*. That year alone, we brought in over a million new consultants.

When I joined the company in 1987 as a speaker and trainer they were doing in the neighborhood of $400,000 a month. By 2007 we were up to $980 million a year, just a stone's throw from a billion.

Was it satisfying to be part of a company that reached the threshold of being a billion-dollar player on the world stage? Sure it was. But what mattered even more to me was what that meant to the individual consultant wanting to carve out a new life for herself. I wanted to make this opportunity available to *anyone*. I wanted it to be a living example of the idea that life is a choice, and that *everyone* has choices—and that this profession was fair to all comers.

In the spring of 2011, after twenty years in the president's chair and nearly twenty-five with the company in one capacity or another, I moved on to step into the next chapter in my life. It was a bittersweet moment; we had accomplished so much together and I was proud of that, and at the same time, I hated to say goodbye. Still, after twenty years of helping people with this one company start a business and put their lives on a path to financial security, success and greater happiness, I was eager to have the opportunity to reach an even wider audience and help more people find their greatest gifts.

When I look back at my years with the cosmetics-and-personal-care company and all the lives we've been able to touch, I always think of Ray. I was so fortunate to discover that in this athletic event called direct selling, I could really *run*—and I know that it all happened only because I had a coach who pushed me into it in the first place.

Thank you forever, Ray … love ya.

The People Who Matter Most

Not long ago I ran into Hugh Downs and his precious wife Ruth at a restaurant not far from where we live. Over the years, Hugh must have had thousands of people come over and shake his hand at restaurant tables, because he was such a well-known face from his long career in broadcasting—the *Today* show for nine years, *Concentration* for eleven years, and *20/20* for more than twenty years. From the sixties through the nineties, there was hardly a more recognizable face on television. What a lot of people don't realize is how versatile he is: he is also an elected member of the National Academy of Sciences, a columnist for *Science Digest*, and on the Board of Governors of the National Space Society. I first got to know Hugh from interviewing him on the show; later on, when I did a special holiday season show from my home, he was kind enough to come and be part of it.

When I saw them I went right over to their table—only rather than approaching Hugh first I reached out my hand to greet Ruth. "Hi, Ruth, I'm Rita Davenport," I said. "We had lunch together in Carefree" (that's a little town not far from

Phoenix) "and I still remember being so tickled when you told our waiter that you like your coffee boiling hot. Do you remember that?"

Now, that had been several decades earlier, and I could see from her face that she couldn't believe I'd remembered that conversation for all those years. "Oh yes," she said, "it's so good to see you."

We visited for a little bit, and then I turned to her husband and said, "Hugh, it's so good to see you, too."

I'll never forget the look on his face. He was positively beaming. It was such a pleasure for him to have someone recognize his wife for a change, and not just him. He knew where his success came from and who mattered most in his life, and it was a joy for him to see that someone else knew it, too.

It's so easy, when someone is famous or accomplished, whether it's the president of the United States, a movie star, or the high school quarterback, for the people around him or her to fade into the background. Typically, though, those same people have had everything to do with helping to create that fame or accomplishment. Every successful person is there only because somewhere in the background there is somebody who supported them, who encouraged them, who enabled them to be that famous person. Ruth is a great example of this. She kept his life balanced, and I don't believe Hugh Downs could have been *Hugh Downs* without Ruth Downs.

Fame is fleeting; wealth is ephemeral; achievements retreat and fade with the advance of time. More than all of these I treasure the connections I've had with the people I love and trust … those who I know have had my back.

Chapter 10

TO FORGIVE IS DIVINELY HUMAN

Remember Saint Rita, the patron saint of lost causes and impossible cases? The more I've gotten to know about her, the more I found we share in common. (No, not the saint part.) For example, Saint Rita had two sons. Hey, I have two sons! Saint Rita was all about helping people who were down on their luck, people in "impossible" situations, to better their lot in life. I'm all about that, too. And look at this: Saint Rita had a Southern accent—and so do I! (Okay, I made that last one up.)

Kidding aside, here's the thing I love most about Saint Rita: along with being the patron saint of impossible causes, she is also the patron saint of *forgiveness*. And I love that because it seems to me that forgiveness is the most hallowed and powerful path to achieving miracles and other "impossibilities" in our lives.

Things have happened to me in the course of my professional life that have been incredibly hurtful. Hurtful things have probably happened to you, too.

I have always tried to take the high road. My dear friend Stasia Trivison once commented, "How do you do it, Rita? You seem to have amnesia to the hurtful things people have said and done to you over time." "Stasia," I replied, "the secret to happiness is good health and a short memory." Still, there have been times when I could easily have cried "Unfair!" and grown bitter about it, yet for some reason, I didn't. At the time, I wasn't even sure why not. But something has always pushed me to look deeper and ask—just as with that time I lost out on the title of high school Band Queen—was there a good reason that this bad thing happened? As I said earlier, with every adversity there is an equal or greater gift.

The answer hasn't always been easy to find. In the case of not making Band Queen, it didn't take long to see the greater good when my high school friend Gail Harmon died a short time later. There have been other times, later in life, when I felt I'd been done wrong and the greater good did not become apparent so quickly, and times when it never became apparent at all.

At times like those, I wonder if it's simply about forgiveness.

I believe the most important thing we have to learn in this life is the capacity to forgive. The most difficult, even horrific circumstances sometimes show up in our lives for no seeming reason and to no perceptible good end. But whether or not we can see it at the time that it happens, there is always a reason, and there is always a good end. If you cannot find any rhyme or reason for why a particular painful or difficult episode in your life should have happened, then take a look at this possibility: perhaps it came about purely as a gift—a gift to help you learn the depth and power of forgiveness.

You know the expression, "To err is human; to forgive is divine"? I love that, but I like to add three more words:

To forgive is divine—and divinely human.

Forgiveness makes for a richer life. It makes you a richer person.

What if you feel you are not a very forgiving person? As they say, practice makes perfect, and even when that is not altogether true it does at least make it *better*.

Let's practice by looking at three specific groups of people to forgive.

Group #1: Forgive Your Parents

I was raised in a home environment that, frankly, was not very nurturing or supportive. I never was hungry, cold, or abused—but I got criticized plenty, put down, and told I'd never amount to much. As tempting as it might be to blame my parents for that, what good would that do? And besides, is it really fair to them? Is it even accurate? When I think back to those times with the perspective of being an adult and a parent myself, knowing how much responsibility and struggle it can be at times and what a stressor the kinds of financial strains they faced can be, it gives me a whole new insight into what they were going through at the time.

I really don't think my parents got together for a cup of coffee in the morning, while we kids were still in bed, and said to each other, "Hey, let's see what we can do today to mess up our kids. How can we make sure they will be wounded and weird for the rest of their lives?" No, I think they were just doing what they could to get through their day. They didn't have parent effectiveness training back then. They didn't have personal development seminars or people teaching them about having an abundance mentality. My parents never had the opportunity to read William James, or Norman Vincent Peale, or Earl Nightingale, or Og Mandino. They didn't have Oprah Winfrey or Dr. Phil giving them counsel on how to support and interact with their kids. For most of us, our parents simply raised us the way *they* were raised, which was all they knew. As Erma put it, they were doing the best they could with the resources they had.

So I have released whatever blame I may have felt toward them—and the rewards have been immense. It has allowed me not only to live with a greater sense of peace, but also to fully enjoy them in the years they were still here.

Ten years after he retired at seventy-six Daddy was suffering from congestive heart failure and the hospital couldn't really do anything for him, so they put him in a rehabilitation facility. It was a very nice place, but he hated it. He'd had a brother who died a fairly ugly death in a nursing home, and he loathed the idea of being in a facility like this.

I'm told that, in the past, when Native Americans sensed the end of life nearing they would go off by themselves and simply withdraw their own life support. Well, Daddy's mother was half–Native American (in fact, in researching my family tree I was surprised to find that we are descended from Pocahontas, an oddly diverse club that includes Nancy Reagan, Woodrow Wilson's wife Edith, and Admiral Richard Byrd), and that's exactly what he did. When he realized he was in a nursing home, even though it was a very nice one, he simply refused all food and water. I would say, "Daddy, take just a sip of water," but he wouldn't. He lived only a few more days. He left this world the same way he lived in this world: firm on his principles.

Nine years later, Mama followed. She was not in perfect health and had complications from diabetes, but she was still basically strong and not suffering or in any pain. Late one night while watching television she simply went to sleep and never woke up. I had spoken with her earlier that evening, and though she usually liked to talk, after only a couple of minutes into our conversation she abruptly said, "I want to go." I protested, saying, "But we just started talking," but she was insistent. Only later did I realize what she was saying: she was letting me know she was ready to leave us. It's comforting to know that those were her last words to me.

I am so grateful that neither one of them suffered. They were good people, and I'm so glad that I was in their lives right up through their final days.

Some people have the philosophy that we choose our parents, our date and time of birth, even our name. We might debate about that (personally, I believe God chooses for us), but I'll tell you what, there is something about it that makes sense to me. Maybe we *do* choose our parents for the specific ideas and experiences we can learn from them.

Dr. Gerald Jampolsky, author of the bestseller *Forgiveness: The Greatest Healer of All*, came on my show as a guest once, and he said something I thought was both wise and beautiful: "Forgiveness is celestial amnesia."

In our conversation he also talked specifically about how important it is to forgive our parents, yet how many people carry around a load of resentment toward their parents. I know people in their fifties, their sixties, heck, in their eighties, who are still holding onto grievances, grudges, and resentments from their childhoods. If you feel that way, you may need to give yourself a mental enema: go to the commode and talk to it, describing the whole incident in detail—and then *flush* it! And never allow that incident to hurt you again.

This goes both ways, too. As parents, we have the opportunity to teach our kids how to forgive. Anytime you can say you're sorry and ask for forgiveness it is a powerful example for your children. Yet how often do we fail to say this to our own family members? As parents, one of the most powerful things we can do is let our kids know that *we* know we made a mistake. "Mama and Daddy made a mistake. We were tired, we were upset, and we're sorry about that now. Would you forgive us?" Kids need to hear that. They need to understand that Mommy and Daddy are real human beings who are not perfect. Even more important, they need to learn that real human beings can admit their mistakes and be forgiven, and that they themselves have the capacity to say, "I forgive you," and that doing this is a powerful thing.

Those people who never take that step of forgiving their own parents? Chances are good they never learned how to forgive from their parents. But if the cycle of bitterness, blame, or even abuse can be passed on from generation to generation, so can the cycle of forgiveness and redemption, and we have the capacity to create that cycle anew anytime we choose to do so.

I know there are plenty of people who have had much tougher childhoods than I, in terms of how their parents treated them. And I can't claim to know what it is like to be someone who suffered total neglect, outright abuse, or violence at the hands of those who were charged with being their protectors. But I do know this: no matter what wrongs have occurred, large or small, forgiveness is always possible, and it brings with it a kind of relief and peace that nothing else can provide.

Group #2: Forgive the People Who've Done You Wrong

My sister Euphiazene once worked with a person who gave her all kinds of trouble. This woman was truly a thorn in her side, and if anyone in Euphiazene's life deserved to be resented, it was her. Furthermore, quite a few other people who worked with her had very similar experiences with her. One year she became ill and went to the hospital. It was easy to see how the people in her life felt about her, because nobody went to visit, and nobody sent flowers. Nobody, that is, except my sister. Euphiazene sent her flowers with a get-well card, and that woman was so grateful that it completely turned around her attitude not only toward my sister but also toward all the other people she worked with.

When someone mistreats us it's usually an indication that they themselves are hurting. Nobody mistreats other people when they feel good about themselves. Have you ever seen a dog seriously hurt, say, in an accident? If you go over to help it, you have to be careful. Even though you're trying to help that animal, it'll snap at you—and if you've ever had a migraine or a really bad toothache, then you know exactly what that's like. When you're in great pain, are you kind and sweet and loving and supportive, just itching to see how you can help others out? No, you're hurting! You're thinking about one thing: getting to a dentist and getting that darn tooth fixed. You are not at your most considerate.

The next time somebody treats you badly, think of that toothache, that migraine, or that injured dog. Pretty soon, instead of thinking, "Why that no-good so-and-so, how can she be so mean?" you'll start thinking, "You poor dear, you need some loving care right now." In the South we always say "Well, bless your heart," whether the person's actions were good or bad.

That little kid who is acting up and turning the classroom into a zoo, he's the one who needs his teacher's love more than anybody else in the room. You don't know what abuse that child is going through at home or what else might be causing that child to behave that way. But you do know this: *you're* the one who is being tested, and even though the child is the one who is acting hostile and causing all kinds of disruption, you're the one who has the capacity to stretch, to reach out and love that child.

I know that's hard. It's harder to love somebody who's treating you badly than it is somebody who's treating you well. But that's exactly what Euphiazene did, and let me tell you, it works.

Whatever happened to you, whoever dumped on you way back whenever, hey, let's forgive them. Do you suppose they are suffering from what happened fourteen years ago? That they are sitting around saying, "Oh, I wish I hadn't done that nasty thing"? Probably not. But every time you ruminate about it or run it back over again in your mind, all you're doing is allowing that person to hurt you one more time. I've heard it said that holding onto anger is like drinking poison and expecting the other person to die.

If somebody has mistreated you, write down what they did to you on a little piece of paper, roll it up, attach it to a helium balloon and wave bye-bye as it soars up and out of sight. Whatever the problem was, it's *over*.

When you release that experience and the person involved, what you are really doing is releasing yourself— because when you hold onto the wrong they've done you, the only person you are truly keeping in chains is *you*.

There Is Good in Everyone
One thing that makes it easier to forgive someone who has

treated you badly is to find some good thing about that person to focus on. "Yeah," you might be saying, "but what if that person is so mean and ornery there *is* nothing good to focus on?"

I know how you feel—but the truth is, no matter how dislikable they may seem, you can *always* find something good if you look hard enough.

The son of a friend of mine, I'll call him "George," worked for a while as a bank teller. One day he happened to look at a "most wanted" list that had been circulated to banks that listed people who were passing bad checks. A few hours later, a man walked up to George's window to cash a check. George immediately recognized him—he was at the top of that Most Wanted list he had just read!

As he began waiting on the man George quietly pushed the silent panic button to summon the police. But a few minutes went by and the police still didn't arrive, so he kept the man engaged in conversation while he feigned trying to complete the transaction. After a few minutes, the teller next to him leaned over and said, "Hey George, what's the holdup?" (By the way, if you are a bank teller, this is probably a phrase you *don't* want to use at work.)

George said, "Well, I've got a problem with my computer."

The fellow said, "Well just send him on over here. My computer's fine and I've got nobody at my window. I can take care of cashing that check for him."

"No," George said, "it'd just mess up my system," and meanwhile he kept trying to signal the other teller with his eyes, but the guy wasn't picking up the clues and persisted in his offer to help the man.

"But I've already entered the transaction," George said, "and I want to go ahead and complete it so I don't mess up my records." The teller left him alone, and he kept chatting with the man as he continued putting on a show of working on his check.

It took a total of eighteen minutes from the time George pushed the panic button until the police arrived, but they finally showed up and apprehended the man, cuffed him, and took him away.

"By the time the police got there, I felt sorry for the guy," George later told his mother when describing the whole scene. "You know, Mom, after talking with him for all that time, he was so likable, I almost wished I hadn't turned him in." If you look closely, you can find good in most *anyone*.

Some People You Just Have to Let Go

Forgiving someone doesn't mean you have to continue suffering their company—and just because George felt sorry for that gentleman and even started to like him doesn't mean they were going to become best buds. I mean, let's get real. The guy was a crook! And by the way, a person doesn't need to be a criminal to be a negative influence you are better off without. Sometimes there are people who are just so consistently negative that the most constructive thing you can do is to bless and release them—to gently but firmly carve them out of your life.

I learned this early on. When David and I were still newly married, I had a coworker I'd often go out with. I adored her, but whenever we got together on a double date, her husband would pick on me unmercifully, making fun of my accent, my education, my background, anything he could find to lampoon. It was painful.

As big a fan of humor and laughter as I am, there is a *big* difference between genuine humor and that brand of sarcastic "humor" that exists only by preying on others. Folks, if you find you have to regularly explain your jokes by saying "I was only kidding," then the person you are kidding is yourself. There's sometimes a fine line between funny and mean-spirited, and if you're not absolutely sure where that line is or how close you are to it, then it's probably a good idea to take three giant steps backward. Jokes and pokes that draw blood are just not funny—and they hurt.

The jokes coming from my friend's husband started as ha-ha fun, but they just kept on and on. Finally I had to explain to my friend that I wasn't going to be able to continue spending time with them. "I love you," I said, "but I'm just not happy being in this kind of critical environment." Life is just too short to let yourself spend time around people who make you feel inferior.

I recently saw an interview with Tom Hanks on television. As Tracy Smith, the interviewer, put it in her introduction, Mr. Hanks has a reputation as "one of the classiest acts in Hollywood."

"You clearly are a guy who's well-liked," said Smith. "Everybody says how much they like Tom Hanks."

"Oh, not everybody," Tom replied. "I think I have a good nature, by and large," he added. "But if someone takes advantage of that good nature, well then, I'm not that nice a guy."

"Do you get mad?" she asked.

"Yeah, sure," he said. "Get mad and either work it out or write 'em off, you know? Look, there's people out there that you *should* write off. There are. I think eighty percent of the population are really great, caring people who will help you and tell you the truth. And I think twenty percent of the population are crooks and liars." He laughed at the reaction that got from some off-camera crew members. "Well, it's just a fact. Am I wrong? I think that's the math. The secret is, find out who the crooks and liars are."

"And that's how you stay so nice—you stay away from them?" asked Smith.

Hanks nodded and said, "I think so."

And I think he is so right. I'd like to believe it's not as many as 20 percent, but there are people who are simply going to be toxic in your life no matter what you do about it. Or as I like to put it, I don't think there are that many truly obnoxious people in the world—but they seem to move around a lot.

My grandmother helped support the family, believe it or not, by raising turkeys. She was quite a character, and I learned a life philosophy from her that has served me well over the years:

Never let the turkeys get you down.

I've known people who were so vicious they could be flight instructors at a broom factory, if you know what I mean. People who almost make you believe in retroactive birth control. Have you ever known people like that? They've got absolutely nothing positive to say about anybody or anything. And let me tell you, one pessimist in the room can pull down ten optimists easier than ten optimists can pull up one pessimist. Sometimes the best solution is simply to leave the room.

Group #3: The Most Important Person to Forgive

As important as it is to forgive your parents, and as valuable as it is to forgive those who have done you wrong, this third group is the most critical of all to forgive. This third group consists of just one person, and I'll bet you have already figured out who that one person is.

Have you ever done something you later regretted? Of course you have; we've all done that. But now let me ask you another question: have you ever done something that you *really, really* regretted? Something you would give anything to go back and undo, something you wish you could travel back in time and jump in to stop yourself from ever doing in the first place?

And if you answered "yes" to that, then I have one more question:

> *Whatever it was you did, however much it may have hurt someone else or however ashamed of it you may have been or may still be today, will you forgive yourself for it, fully and completely, right now?*

Someone far greater than you or I once said, "Forgive them, Father"—and he was talking about the people who were in the process of killing him! So what's keeping you from forgiving yourself?

Self-blame is one of the greatest paralytic forces that choke off people's dreams like a poison, and self-forgiveness is the only antidote.

From here on out, I want to ask you to keep this thought always in the back of your mind: If you did something that you're sorry about, that you're ashamed of, that you wish you had never done and would take back if you could, would you understand one thing? With your awareness at the time, *you did the best you could.*

"No I didn't," you might say. "I could have done better. I could have done this instead, or I could have refrained from doing that." Sure, you can say so now, but that's in retrospect. It's always easy to see things with clarity when you're looking backward. Hindsight is always 20/20. But that's Monday-morning quarterbacking: you're judging the actions of the past with the eyes of the present. Whatever you did back then that you're sorry for right now, with your consciousness at the time, you made the best judgment that you possibly could.

That was then, and you're a new person now. Because honestly, you're a new person in every new moment. It's time to start forgiving yourself.

It may not feel like it, because it tends to become such an ingrained habit of thought that we stop being aware of it, but self-recrimination takes a ton of energy. Walking around with a burden of self-blame is like running a race with heavy ankle-weights on. And when you take those weights off, it is amazing how light you feel. When you truly forgive yourself, it profoundly affects your confidence and self-esteem—and what's more, it is the only way you can really become accomplished at forgiving other people.

In that way, forgiveness is like love. How can you truly love another if you cannot love yourself? And how can you forgive others if you have not yet embraced forgiving yourself?

Quit beating yourself up. Decide to love yourself. Choose to forgive yourself. Then, and *only* then, will you be able to look around you in this world and start to find a new level of greatness in others and find new qualities to love in those around you, because you'll no longer be using that big chunk of your consciousness to continue judging yourself.

Self-forgiveness is not a one-time event. Because there is so much negativity in our environment, this is something I believe we need to work on continually. It means developing the habit of standing in front of the mirror (I'm speaking figuratively here) and saying to yourself, "I'm worthy, I'm loving, I'm kind. I have messed up in the past, but I was doing the best I could, and I am fundamentally a good human being who wants the best for others as well as for myself."

Stop holding yourself hostage to whatever chorus of self-condemnation you may have playing in your head. Be as compassionate toward yourself as you are toward the people you care about most. That's the only way you will fully unfurl your wings and spread out those gifts that you were given to share with the world.

There is only one of you, and we need you. So don't keep your light buried under a bushel of self-blame and regret. Set yourself free. Let yourself live a big life.

Learn to Receive

You've probably noticed by now that the word *forgive* contains the word *give*, and it's quite true: forgiveness is another type of giving and another type of gift. I've talked earlier about how important it is to give, but now I want to talk about another side of giving that people often miss.

There is a secret to being a giving person that even the nicest, most giving people may never learn how to master, and that, if you do master it, will help to make you a far *more* giving person. Are you ready? Here it is:

To be a genuinely giving person, you have to be willing to receive.

I can go up to you and say, "You look so great today," and if you're like most people you'll say something like, "Oh, no, I feel terrible, actually, I just flew in from the coast last night and I still have jet lag, I'm exhausted." Hey, they didn't want to hear all that. They were just trying to say something nice—and you rejected it! (As I like to say, "Don't tell people your problems; half of them don't want to hear about it, and the other half think you deserve it.")

Or I'll say, "That's the prettiest dress," and you reply, "Oh, this old rag?" Why do we do this? Because we're not letting ourselves receive. Perhaps it's because we feel we don't deserve it, that deep down inside we're really not good people. Maybe we bought the package someone sold us when we were young and vulnerable, that old battered self-esteem still buying into the story that we don't deserve to be happy, appreciated, acknowledged, and valued. Perhaps it's fueled by some sense of residual guilt we have over things we've done, or imagine we've done.

Whatever it is, get over it. Let it go. Because if you can't receive a simple compliment, how will you ever be able to receive the larger blessings that life has in store for you? Sometimes that same feeling of unworthiness can lead us to sabotage the greatest opportunities that come into our lives. Give yourself permission to receive fully, to accept and enjoy.

When somebody compliments you, the best thing you can say is "Why, thank you! Thank you for that." Why is that so hard? I'll tell you why: because we have an ingrained habit of resisting instead of receiving gracefully and fully. It's like my friends Bob Burg and John David Mann say in *The Go-Giver*:

> All the giving in the world won't bring success,
> won't create the results you want, unless
> you also make yourself willing and able to
> receive in like measure. Because if you don't
> let yourself receive, you're refusing the gifts of
> others—and you shut down the flow.[13]

In order to receive fully and gracefully you have to feel *worthy* to receive, because you will only receive what you genuinely believe you deserve. And it is only when you allow yourself to fully receive what life is sending your way that you will be able to fully give back to the world all that you're capable of giving.

Eat Dessert First

There is something ironic about life. It is so precious and so valuable—but the only way to experience how precious it is, is to *live* it, and in the act of living it, you are using it up. You don't get yesterday back. This is not a dress rehearsal. There are no do-overs. This, right now, this is your life.

We get so caught up in our work and the tasks of life that we don't get outside to simply sit down on the grass and feel all the wonderful elements that are there for us to enjoy. Some people say success is getting what you want. But what good is success if you don't take the time to enjoy what you've received? If you ask me, genuine success is more about enjoying what you have—and I've seen a lot of people who managed to fulfill that first definition (getting what they wanted) but never got around to the second (enjoying it).

I like to spend time with my kids and grandkids. I like to go fishing, to go horseback riding, to hike, to watch the sunset, to watch the sunrise, to hear the birds singing in the early morning. I like to cook and entertain. These things make me happy, so I do them whenever I can. Doing them makes me a happier person, and that makes me a better bringer of joy to the people around me.

What truly makes you happy? What is it that you really like to do but that you've been putting off? Do it now. Make that trip you've been planning on but haven't gotten around to taking. Don't put these things off any longer. Seek out those activities that will make you happy, and start doing them *now*. It's time to give yourself that gift. It may not be good practice in nutritional terms, but in terms of the experiences of life, *eat dessert first*. If you put it all off for later, you may find that later is never.

Every Moment Is So Precious

One morning many years ago, my dear friend Margie Williams' husband Dale was getting ready to go to work. They had been married nine years, Margie says, but were still madly in love. "We still had the passion," she says. That morning, however, he had been a little grumpy with her. Before leaving, Dale took a moment to apologize for his grouchiness. They told each other they loved each other and kissed just before he walked out the door. Dale was thirty-two years old and seemingly in perfect health ... yet he dropped dead of a heart attack that morning before reaching his car.

Sometime after Dale's death, when I was on a visit home to Nashville, I had lunch with Margie and we talked about what had happened. She told me that she was so incredibly grateful that they had taken those few moments to kiss and make up, and that their last words had been words of love. Dale was only thirty-two. How could either of them have possibly known these would be their last few moments together?

How do any of us know? We don't. Life is as transitory as a wisp of smoke from a distant chimney. The Bible says that each human being is like a vapor, our days like a fleeting shadow. It all goes by so fast.

Billy Graham was a guest on my show once and said something that made a big impression on me. "You know what shocks me most about life, Rita? Its brevity."

The most important truth about having a rich life is this: *every single one of us already has an incredibly rich life.* Sometimes there are feelings and issues that may stand in the way of our appreciating or realizing that fact, but it's there nonetheless. What an amazing, miraculous thing life is. That we are here, that we can breathe this air, see and hear, touch and feel, love one another and support one another in all our uniqueness ... it's really quite breathtaking. Every moment is so precious. Yet too often, we don't notice this—and really, every moment we overlook the miraculous nature of our lives is a wasted moment that we cannot ever get back.

There's been a lot of criticism lately about how wasteful our society is, and certainly there is a significant amount of truth to that. We do waste energy, water, food, yes ... but I believe these things all pale in comparison with the wasted moments, moments when we could be basking in the glory of each other's humanity and sharing our love with others, yet fail to do so. If you just waste ten minutes today, that doesn't seem like much. But if you do that every day, you know what that adds up to in a year? Sixty hours—one whole forty-hour work week plus half of another.

How important is ten minutes? Not that important, right? But what if you're ten minutes late for your own wedding? Imagine if you had a chance to talk to someone like Benjamin Franklin or Thomas Jefferson. I would do almost anything to have ten minutes to talk to someone like that.

What if one of your parents or grandparents were dying in a hospital and you were rushing to their side to tell them how much you loved them, and you got there ten minutes too late? I would give anything to have ten more minutes right now with my grandmother, to sit and hold her hand and talk to her. Well, I don't have my grandmother here—but I do have those ten precious minutes to do with as I choose. Why would I want to waste them by filling them with regret, bitching and moaning, or feeling sorry for myself?

If you knew for an absolute fact that you had only five minutes left to live, how do you suppose you would spend those five minutes? You suppose you would grab the nearest telephone and call up that person who did you wrong twenty-five years ago and chew them out? Say, "You know, I am still mighty sore about what you did. Come to think of it, I never have liked you anyway, and I just wanted you to know that."

No, of course you wouldn't. You'd grab the nearest phone, call the person who means the most to you, and say, "I love you, and I wanted you to know that."

A Rich Life

I have a girlfriend who married a very wealthy man, and for a wedding present he gave her a brand new Rolls-Royce. She was so excited about that car. One day she pulled up to my house to take me out to lunch, and when I climbed in she said, "Tell me, Rita, with your impoverished background, did you ever think you'd get to ride in a Rolls-Royce?"

"Not in the front seat," I said.

Funny thing: she never brought up her Rolls again.

Many people think that success is wealth, but you and I both know that's not true. When I talk about having a *rich life*, I don't mean just rich materially. Some of the richest people I know are some of the most miserable. And some of the poorest people I know, financially, are the richest in love, enthusiasm, wonder, excitement, and joy. Success doesn't stem from money or material wealth. In fact, it's actually the exact other way around. The trappings of comfort and material fulfillment are a natural expression of a rich life: a life spent in the pursuit of learning and love.

Money isn't everything—although I do think it's right up there with oxygen. And don't get me wrong: I don't have a thing against anybody wanting to be being rich materially. I kid about my friend and her Rolls-Royce, but you know, good for her. It's been said that money won't make you happy, and that's true. Tell you what, though, neither will poverty. Frank Sinatra said, "I've been rich and I've been poor, and rich is better." I agree with that 100 percent. But the biggest reason I would rather be materially prosperous than materially poor is that if I have more resources, then I can do a lot more for a lot more people than if I had to beg others for those resources.

What makes a rich life?

I've looked at it a lot of ways, spent my entire life studying that question from different angles, interviewed hundreds of celebrities and tremendously successful people on my television show, helped thousands of people create their own success in business, spent thousands of hours with the poorest of the poor in the backwaters of Florida, and dined with the richest of the rich. And here's my conclusion:

What makes a life genuinely rich is most accurately measured by how many ways you make a positive difference in other people's lives.

We are, each of us, here for such a short time. Our lives are indeed a vapor. In the brief moments we have here on earth, how many lives can we touch, and how many people can we help uplift? How many can you take with you as you climb to the top?

Recommended Reading

Allen, James: *As a Man Thinketh*. First ed. 1903; rev. ed., Tarcher, 2008.

Barrett, Tom: *Dare to Dream and Work to Win: Understanding the Dollars and Sense in Network Marketing*. Thomas J. Barrett, 1998.

Blanchard, Kenneth H., and Spencer Johnson, M.D.: *The One Minute Manager*. William Morrow, 1982.

Bombeck, Erma: *The Grass Is Always Greener Over the Septic Tank*. McGraw-Hill, 1976.

—*If Life Is a Bowl of Cherries, What Am I Doing in the Pits?* McGraw-Hill, 1978.

Bristol, Claude M.: *The Magic of Believing*. First ed. 1948; rereleased, Prentice Hall Press, 1984.

Brown, Les: *It's Not Over Till You Win: How to Become the Person You Always Wanted to Be No Matter What the Obstacle*. Simon & Schuster, 1997.

Burg, Bob, and John David Mann: *The Go-Giver: A Little Story About a Powerful Business Idea*. Portfolio, 2008.

—*Go-Givers Sell More*. Portfolio, 2010.

—*It's Not About You: A Little Story About What Matters Most in Business*. Portfolio, 2011.

Canfield, Jack: *The Success Principles: How to Get From Where You Are to Where You Want to Be*. William Morrow, 2004.

Carnegie, Dale: *How to Win Friends and Influence People*. First ed. 1936; rev. ed., Simon & Schuster, 2009.

Cilley, Marla: *Sink Reflections*. Random House, 2002.

Cole-Whittaker, Terry: *What You Think of Me Is None of My Business*. First ed. 1979; paperback ed., Jove, 1988.

Dyer, Wayne: *You'll See It When You Believe It: The Way to Your Personal Transformation*. William Morrow & Co., 1989.

Hansen, Mark Victor, and Robert G. Allen: *The One Minute Millionaire: The Enlightened Way to Wealth*. Harmony Books, 2002.

Helmstetter, Shad: *The Gift: The 12 Greatest Tools of Personal Growth—and How to Put Them Into Practice*, foreword by Rita Davenport. Park Avenue Press, 2005.

—*What to Say When You Talk to Yourself*. First ed. 1986; paperback Pocket Books, 1990.

Hill, Napoleon: *Think and Grow Rich*. First ed. 1937; rev. ed., Random House.

James, William: *The Will to Believe and Other Essays in Popular Philosophy*. The New World, Volume 5, 1896.

Jampolsky, Gerald: *Forgiveness: The Greatest Healer of All*. Atria Books/Beyond Words, 1999.

Julian, Larry S.: *God Is My CEO: Following God's Principles in a Bottom-Line World*. Adams Media, 2002.

Larson, Joe: *My Ph.D. in Living*. Value Network, 2002.

Lechter, Sharon L. and Greg S. Reid: *Three Feet from Gold: Turn Your Obstacles into Opportunities*. Sterling, 2009.

LeHew, Calvin, and Stowe Dailey Shockey: *Flying High*, forewords by Naomi Judd and Rita Davenport. 2011. Available from www.flyinghighbook.com.

Leonard, George: *Mastery: The Keys to Success and Long-Term Fulfillment*. Dutton, 1991.

Mackay, Harvey: *Dig Your Well Before You're Thirsty: The Only Networking Book You'll Ever Need*. Crown Business, 1997.

Mandino, Og: *The Greatest Salesman in the World.* Bantam Books, 1974.

Maxwell, John: *Developing the Leader Within You.* Thomas Nelson, 2000.

McGraw, Phillip: *Self Matters: Creating Your Life from the Inside Out.* Free Press, 2001.

Moody, Raymond A.: *Life After Life.* Mockingbird Books, 1981.

Nightingale, Earl: *The Strangest Secret.* Audio ed., Nightingale Conant, 1956, 1986.

Osteen, Joel: *Your Best Life Now: 7 Steps to Living at Your Full Potential.* Warner Faith, 2004.

Pausch, Randy, and Jeffrey Zaslow: *The Last Lecture.* Hyperion, 2008.

Stockett, Kathryn: *The Help.* Putnam, 2009.

Warren, Rick: *The Purpose-Driven Life: What on Earth Am I Here For?* Zondervan, 2002.

Acknowledgements

It's been a while since my last book, though I've often been urged to share my continually positive approach to life and all that it throws at us.

The catalyst, though, that created a compelling call to action, was a call I received from my friend Sandra Tillinghast. Barely awake from anesthesia after surgery for a double mastectomy, she said, "Rita, I had to call. I woke up from surgery realizing you're supposed to do something even bigger." Good grief! I'd been worried about her, and here she was giving *me* needed encouragement.

As it happened, I'd also been approached earlier by another friend, Stuart Johnson, president and CEO of *SUCCESS* magazine and Video Plus, to collaborate on a book endeavor supported by trainings all over the world. The project had stayed in the back of my mind, and after Sandra's call it now became compelling.

So here it is at last, finally finished—with gratitude to the tens of thousands of you who have helped make my life what it is today through your love, support, encouragement, and example. Much of what I've learned has been the result of your insight.

This book would not have become a reality without the help and support of some very creative, important, and pivotal people in my life who each demonstrated a commitment to excellence, and I'd like to thank them.

First, my thanks and admiration for his creativity and patience to my coauthor John David Mann. In 2006 John created a character in one of his best-selling books, *The Go-Giver*, who was a speaker named Debra Davenport. Later he acknowledged that, yes, my way of speaking and engaging an audience had influenced the character. God winked, and years later I got to spend time with this amazing man. Though he is a composer, musician, entrepreneur, and writer, he never made me feel anything but *special*. I've nicknamed him Sweetheart Darling, my mother's favorite

Southern term of endearment.

My thanks also to those folks who read unedited versions of the manuscript and gave their wisdom and heartfelt encouragement, including my sister Euphiazene and her husband Lucion, my precious friends Joe and Jan Larson, Linda and Phil Dowdy, Tom Helms, David Studnicki, Sandi Hveem, Margie Aung-Khin, Sharon Lechter, Stasia Trivison, and Jodi Whittemore, Sharon Metzgar, Pierre O'Rourke, Thomas Tidlund, and Donna Johnson.

Next I must give special thanks to my friend David Vermillion, who types faster than the speed of light, for recording my mile-a-minute ideas, dictation, and edits, whether early in the morning or after midnight.

Kudos to the entire team at *SUCCESS* and Video Plus, which includes Reed Bilbray, Steve Jamieson, Steve Norton, Sam Watson and Meridith Simes, for their creativity, direction, editing, and support. All in all, the best team around!

To all my family, friends, peers, colleagues, and staff who, I regret, I cannot take the space here to list individually, my deepest thanks for challenging me to raise the bar by creating an unforgettable message. Your feedback on my effort to impact the world is gratifying. I love you all dearly.

Notes

1 Gorman, James, "Scientists Hint at Why Laughter Feels So Good." *New York Times*, September 13, 2011. Retrieved February 14, 2012: http://www.nytimes.com/2011/09/14/science/14laughter.html

2 Peeples, Lynn, "Laughter, Music May Lower Blood Pressure." *CNN Health*, March 28, 2011. Retrieved February 14, 2012: http://www.cnn.com/2011/HEALTH/03/25/laughter.music.lower.blood.pressure/index.html

3 Park, Madison, "Can Laughing Give You a Workout?" *CNN Health*, April 28, 2010. Retrieved February 14, 2012: http://articles.cnn.com/2010-04-28/health/laughter.health.benefits_1_lee-berk-leptin-small-new-study?_s=PM:HEALTH

4 Conversations with the author; also Maza, Michael, "Editha Merrill Flies the Hard Way." *People*, December 12, 1983. Retrieved: February 14, 2012: http://www.people.com/people/archive/article/0,,20086548,00.html

5 Rosenthal, Robert and Lenore Jacobson, *Pygmalion in the Classroom: Teacher Expectation and Pupils' Intellectual Development*. Irvington Publishers: New York, 1992.

6 Rhem, James, "Pygmalion in the Classroom," *National Teaching & Learning Forum*, February 1999, Vol. 8 No. 2; retrieved: February 14, 2012: http://www.ntlf.com/html/pi/9902/pygm_1.htm

7 James, William, *Familiar Letters of William James*, 2nd installment, James, Henry, Ed. *The Atlantic Monthly*, August 1920. Retrieved February 14, 2012: http://www.theatlantic.com/past/docs/issues/96may/nitrous/jamii.htm

8   Burg, Bob and John David Mann, *Go-Givers Sell More.* Portfolio: New York 2010, p. 18.

9   Nerem, R.M., et al., "Social Environment as a Factor in Diet-Induced Atherosclerosis." *Science* 208 (1980); 1475–6, quoted in Dossey, Larry, M.D., *Space, Time, and Medicine.* Boston: Shambala Publications, 1982.

10   cummings, e.e., "A Poet's Advice to Students." *E. E. Cummings, A Miscellany.* New York: Argophile Press, 1955, p. 13.

11   From the "parable of the faithful servant," Luke 12:35–48 (NJKV).

12   Proverbs 17:22 (NASB).

13   Burg, Bob, and John David Mann, *The Go-Giver.* New York: Portfolio 2008, p. 108.

Appendix

RITAISMS

The following is an abbreviated selection of one-liners submitted by Rita's long-time followers—memorable things they have heard her say over the years that have had an impact on their lives. Some are profound, some are funny, some are just plain silly—and all are 100 percent Rita.

WHO YOU ARE

Success is living the life you choose.

We need to love ourselves before we love others.

When we believe in ourselves, the possibilities are endless.

God didn't make any junk.

Don't ever let anyone tell you that you
can't get above your raising.

Don't hang around with people who are
more messed up than you are.

ATTITUDE

Don't *should* on yourself.

Keep calm and carry on.

Give yourself a mental enema.

Ask yourself, is this a hill you want to die on?

Put your big girl panties on and deal with it!

BUSINESS

Money isn't everything, but it's right up there with oxygen.

Know that you are at the right place, at the right time,
with the right opportunity, and the right products.

When someone says *no* that just means
they don't *know* enough yet.

We are not dope dealers, we're *hope* dealers.

You have to circulate to percolate.

Get your *ask* in gear.

Be more, have more, learn more, and
earn more so you can share more.

Take your business seriously, but don't
take yourself too seriously.

When you're working hard on your business,
don't forget to take care of your husband—
because if you don't, someone else will.

There is nothing sexier than a rich woman—and
I remind my husband of that frequently.

LIFE

Do a little more than is expected of you.

A handout is not as good as a hand up.

The secret to happiness is good health and a short memory.

If money will fix it, it's not a problem.

Rewards are in proportion to our service.

Love what is.

About the Authors

Rita Davenport

Rita Davenport is an internationally recognized expert in the principles of success, time management, goal-setting, creative thinking, and self-esteem and confidence. Her unique background as an entrepreneur, corporate executive, author, speaker, humorist, and broadcaster sets her apart and has made her one of the most beloved and widely admired role models on the speaking circuit.

She produced and hosted her own award-winning television shows in Phoenix, Arizona, for 15 years. The Arizona Broadcasters Association inducted her into their Hall of Fame. She has also appeared as a guest on more than 200 radio and television shows, including ABC's *Good Morning America*, NBC's *The Today Show*, *Lifestyles with Regis Philbin*, and *The Sally Jesse Raphael Show*.

As a speaker, Rita has been called motivational, challenging, humorous, personal, and powerful. She is a charter member of the National Speakers Association and is listed in the NSA Hall of Fame, and has shared the speakers' platform with such notables as Erma Bombeck, Les Brown, Jack Canfield, Dr. Wayne Dyer, Mark Victor Hansen, Tom Hopkins, John Maxwell, Og Mandino, Denis Waitley, and Zig Ziglar. She has presented over 1,000 seminars globally and been retained as a management consultant to *Fortune* 500 companies.

Rita has written three books that have sold over one million copies, including the bestseller *Making Time, Making Money* and two cookbooks, *Sourdough Cookery* and *De Grazia & Mexican Cookery*, with famed Southwestern artist Ted De Grazia.

An accomplished entrepreneur, promoting *Success*

Strategies, Rita was a pioneer in the field of personal-development infomercials, producing two highly successful programs in the late eighties based on her audio programs, *It's Time for You* and *Laugh Your Way to Success,* which were viewed in over 32 million homes. In 1991 she was named president of Arbonne International, a personal care products company. Under her twenty-year leadership, Arbonne experienced tremendous growth and recognition in the direct sales industry, growing from a $4.5 million company to nearly $1 billion in annual sales and well more than a million independent representatives. Her story has been featured in many national magazines, such as *SUCCESS, People, Networking Times,* and *Working at Home.*

The first person in her family ever to graduate from high school, Rita went on to earn a B.S. degree from Middle Tennessee State University and in 1984 was honored with its Distinguished Alumnus Award. She has been named an Outstanding Young Woman in America and been honored as Arizona's Woman of the Year. She has taught at both high school and graduate levels in Daytona Beach, Florida, and Phoenix, Arizona. Rita has also been involved in many professional organizations including the Direct Selling Association, Platform Professionals, American Women in Radio and Television, Arizona Press Women, and Women in Communications, and has been an active philanthropist, especially in her work to support Sojourner Center and Faces In The Mirror in Phoenix, Arizona.

Rita feels that her most outstanding accomplishments have been as wife to her high school sweetheart, David, and mother to her two sons, Michael and Scott. She resides in Scottsdale, Arizona, with her husband.

 www.RitaDavenport.com

 www.facebook.com/OfficialRitaDavenport

John David Mann

John has been creating careers since he was recipient of the 1969 BMI Awards to Student Composers; at age 17, he and a few friends started their own high school in Orange, New Jersey, called Changes. In 1986 he founded *Solstice*, a journal on health and environmental issues. In 1992 he produced *The Greatest Networker in the World*, by John Milton Fogg, which sold over one

million copies. During the 1990s, he built a multimillion-dollar direct sales organization of over 100,000 people. He was cofounder and senior editor of *Upline* and editor in chief of *Network Marketing Lifestyles* and *Networking Times*.

John is coauthor with Bob Burg of the national bestseller, *The Go-Giver, Go-Givers Sell More*, and *It's Not About You*. He also coauthored the *New York Times* bestseller *Flash Foresight* with Daniel Burrus, the *New York Times* bestseller *The Red Circle* with Brandon Webb, *Code To Joy* with George Pratt, PhD, and Peter Lambrou, PhD, *Take the Lead* with Betsy Myers, and *The Secret Language of Money* with David Krueger, M.D. His writing credits also include *The Answer* by John Assaraf and Murray Smith, *The Next Millionaires* by Paul Zane Pilzer, *The Slight Edge* by Jeff Olson, and *The Business of the 21st Century* by Robert Kiyosaki. In 2007 he published *The Zen of MLM*, a collection of his writings from the past two decades.

His writing has earned the Nautilus Book Award, the Axiom Business Book Award (Gold Medal), and Taiwan's Golden Book Award for Innovation.

He is married to Ana Gabriel Mann and considers himself the luckiest mann in the world.

   www.JohnDavidMann.com

   www.facebook.com/JohnDavidMann

Resource Guide

SUCCESS

What *Achievers* Read™

Your monthly supply of new ideas, inspiration, and resources that will continue to give you the competitive advantage in life. Each magazine comes with a SUCCESS CD, featuring interviews with Darren Hardy and today's greatest achievers and leading success experts.

www.SUCCESS.com/subscribe

SUCCESS
BOOK SUMMARIES

SUCCESS Book Summaries provide a sneak peek at the content of each featured book, with a special focus on chapters that resonate with entrepreneurs and achievers. With a subscription to SUCCESS Book Summaries, you'll receive summaries of three featured books in printed, audio, and PDF formats each month. By reading and listening to the summaries, you'll know whether the books are titles you'd like to add to your personal success library. Listen, read, and achieve more!

www.SUCCESSBookSummaries.com

Go to www.SUCCESS.com for more information.